Student Study Guide and Solutions Manual for
COLLEGE PHYSICS

Taken from:

Student Study Guide and Solutions Manual, Fifth Edition
by Bo Lou

for *College Physics*, Fifth Edition
by Wilson and Buffa

PEARSON
Custom
Publishing

PEARSON
Prentice
Hall

Taken from:

Student Study Guide and Solutions Manual
by Bo Lou
for *College Physics,* Fifth Edition
by Wilson and Buffa
Copyright © 2003 Pearson Education, Inc.
Published by Pearson Prentice Hall
Upper Saddle River, NJ 07458

Printed in the United States of America

10 9 8 7 6 5 4 3 2

ISBN 0-536-91986-0

2005360336

LB

Please visit our web site at *www.pearsoncustom.com*

PEARSON CUSTOM PUBLISHING
75 Arlington Street, Suite 300, Boston, MA 02116
A Pearson Education Company

Table of Contents

CHAPTER 1

Measurement and Problem Solving

I.   Chapter Objectives

Upon completion of this chapter, you should be able to:

1.   distinguish standard units and system of units.

2.   describe the SI and specify the references for the three main base quantities of this system.

3.   use common metric prefixes and nonstandard metric units.

4.   explain the advantage of and apply dimensional analysis and unit analysis.

5.   explain conversion-factor relationships and apply them in converting units within a system or from one system of units to another.

6.   determine the number of significant figures in a numerical value and report the proper number of significant figures after performing simple calculations.

7.   establish a problem-solving procedure and apply it to typical problems.

II.   Chapter Summary and Discussion

1.   International System of Units (SI) (Sections 1.1 – 1.3)

Objects and phenomena are measured and described using **standard units**, a group of which make up a **system of units**.

(1)   The International System of Units (SI), or the metric system, has only seven base quantities (see Table 1.1). The base units for the base quantities length, mass, and time are the **meter** (m), the **kilogram** (kg), and the **second** (s), respectively. A derived quantity (unit) is a combination of the base quantity (units). For example, the units of the derived quantity speed, **meters per second**, are a combination of **meter** and **second**. There are many derived units.

(2)   The metric system is a base–10 (decimal) system, which is very convenient for changing measurements from one unit to another. Metric multiples are designated by prefixes, the most common of which are **kilo–** (1000), **centi–** (1/100), and **milli–** (1/1000). For example, a centimeter is 1/100 of a meter. A complete list of the metric prefixes is given in Table 1.2. A unit of volume or capacity is the **liter** (L), and 1 L = 1000 mL = 1000 cm^3 (cubic centimeters).

2. Dimensional Analysis (Section 1.4)

The fundamental or base quantities, such as length, mass, and time are called **dimensions**. These are commonly expressed by the bracketed symbols [L], [M], and [T], respectively. **Dimensional analysis** is a procedure by which the dimensional correctness of an equation may be checked or the dimensions of derived quantities can be found. Both sides of an equation must be equal not only in numerical value but also in dimension. Dimensions can be treated like algebraic quantities. For example, $[L] \times [L] = [L^2]$ and $\frac{[L]}{[T^2]} \times [T] = [L]/[T]$. Instead of dimensional symbols, units may be used in **unit analysis**, such as $m \times m = m^2$ and $\frac{m}{s^2} \times s = m/s$.

Dimensional analysis can be used to

(1) check whether an equation is **dimensionally correct**, i.e., if an equation has the same dimension (unit) on both sides.

(2) find out the dimension or units of derived quantities.

Example 1.1: Check whether the equation $x = at^2$ is dimensionally correct, where x is length, a is acceleration, and t is time interval.

Solution:

The dimensions and units of x, a, and t, are [L], m; $\frac{[L]}{[T^2]}$, m/s^2; and [T], s; respectively.

Dimensional analysis: Dimension of left side of the equation is [L].

Dimension of right side of the equation is $\frac{[L]}{[T^2]} \times [T^2] = [L]$.

Therefore, the dimension of the left side is equal to the dimension of the right side, and the equation is dimensionally correct. *Note: Dimensionally correct does not necessarily mean the equation is correct.* For example, the "equation" 2 tables = 3 tables, is dimensionally correct but not numerically correct.

Unit analysis: Units of the left side are m.

Units of the right side are $(m/s^2)(s)^2 = m$.

Thus, the units of the left side are equal to the units of the right side, and the equation is dimensionally correct.

Example 1.2: Einstein's famous statement of energy–mass equivalence says that the rest energy of a mass is equal to its mass times the speed of light squared. Determine the dimension and units of energy.

Solution:

Because energy is equal to mass times speed squared, the dimension (units) of energy must be equal to the dimension (units) of mass times the dimension (units) of speed squared.

Thus, the dimension of energy is $[M] \times \left(\dfrac{[L]}{[T]} \right)^2 = \dfrac{[M] \cdot [L^2]}{[T^2]}$,

and the units of energy are $kg \times (m/s)^2 = kg \cdot m^2/s^2$, which is defined as joule (J).

3. Unit Conversions (Section 1.5)

A quantity may be expressed in other units through the use of **conversion factors** such as $\dfrac{1\ mi}{1609\ m} = 1$ or

$\dfrac{1609\ m}{1\ mi} = 1$. Note that any conversion factor is equal to 1 (because 1 mi = 1609 m, for example) and so they can multiply or divide any quantity without altering the quantity. The appropriate form of a conversion factor is easily determined by dimensional (unit) analysis. The same process can be generalized to multiple conversions, as in the case of converting meters per second (m/s) to miles per hour (mi/h) shown in Example 1.4.

Example 1.3: A jogger walks 3200 m every day. What is this distance in miles?

Solution:

Here we need to convert meters to miles. We can accomplish this by using the conversion factor $\dfrac{1\ mi}{1609\ m}$.

The resultant units will be $m \times \dfrac{mi}{m} = mi$.

We do not multiply by $\dfrac{1609\ m}{1\ mi}$ because the resultant units would be $m \times \dfrac{m}{mi} = m^2/mi$, which are incorrect.

$(3200\ m) \times 1 = (3200\ m) \times \dfrac{1\ mi}{1609\ m} = 1.99\ mi \approx 2.0\ mi$. (Here $\dfrac{1\ mi}{1609\ m} = 1$.)

Note the cancellation of the units m, which yields the desired result.

Example 1.4: A car travels with a speed of 25 m/s. What is this speed in mi/h (miles per hour)?

Solution:

Here we need to convert meters to miles *and* seconds to hours. We can use the conversion factor $\dfrac{1 \text{ mi}}{1609 \text{ m}}$

to convert meters to miles, and $\dfrac{3600 \text{ s}}{1 \text{ h}}$ to convert 1/s to 1/h.

[Why can't we multiply by $\dfrac{1 \text{ h}}{3600 \text{ s}}$?]

$$(25 \text{ m/s}) \times 1 \times 1 = (25 \text{ m/s}) \times \frac{1 \text{ mi}}{1609 \text{ m}} \times \frac{3600 \text{ s}}{1 \text{ h}} = 56 \text{ mi/h}.$$

We can also use the direct conversion (1 mi/h = 0.447 m/s).

$$(25 \text{ m/s}) \times \frac{1 \text{ mi/h}}{0.447 \text{ m/s}} = 56 \text{ mi/h}.$$

4. Significant Figures (Section 1.6)

The number of **significant figures** (sf) in a quantity is the number of reliably known digits it contains. For example, the quantity 15.2 m has 3 sf, 0.052 kg has 2 sf, and 3.0 m/s has 2 sf. In general,

- *the final result of a multiplication and/or division should have the same number of significant figures as the quantity with the least number of significant figures used in the calculation,* and
- *the final result of an addition and/or subtraction should have the same number of decimal places as the quantity with the least number of decimal places used in the calculation.*

The proper number of figures or digits is obtained by rounding off a result. Generally, if the digit to be dropped is 5 or greater, increase the preceding digit by one. For example, round 23.46 to 23.5.

Example 1.5: Perform the following operations, and write the answer with the correct numbers of significant figures.

(a) $0.586 \times 3.4 =$

(b) $13.90 \div 0.580 =$

(c) $(13.59 \times 4.86) \div 2.1 =$

(d) $4.8 \times 10^5 \div 4.0 \times 10^{-3} =$

(e) $(3.2 \times 10^8)(4.0 \times 10^4) =$

Solution:

The final result of the multiplication and/or division should have the same number of significant figures as the quantity with the least number of significant figures.

(a) $0.586 \times 3.4 = 2.0$ (not 1.99).

(b) $13.90 \div 0.580 = 24.0$ (not 23.96).

(c) $13.59 \times 4.86 \div 2.1 = 31$ (not 31.45).

(d) $4.8 \times 10^5 \div 4.0 \times 10^{-3} = 1.2 \times 10^8$ (not 1.20×10^8).

(e) $(3.2 \times 10^8)(4.0 \times 10^4) = 1.3 \times 10^{13}$ (not 1.28×10^{13}).

Example 1.6: Perform the following operations, and write the answers with the correct number of significant figures.

(a) $23.1 + 45 + 0.68 + 100 = 169$

(b) $157 - 5.689 + 2 = 153$

(c) $23.5 + 0.567 + 0.85 = 25$

(d) $4.69 \times 10^{-6} - 2.5 \times 10^{-5} =$

(e) $8.9 \times 10^4 + 2.5 \times 10^5 =$

Solution:

The final result of the addition and/or subtraction should have the same number of decimal places as the quantity with the least number of decimal places.

(a) $23.1 + 45 + 0.68 + 100 = 169$ (not 168.8).

(b) $157 - 5.689 + 2 = 153$ (not 153.3).

(c) $23.5 + 0.567 + 0.85 = 24.9$ (not 24.92).

(d) $4.69 \times 10^{-6} - 2.5 \times 10^{-5} = 0.469 \times 10^{-5} - .5 \times 10^{-5} = -2.0 \times 10^{-5}$ (not -2.03×10^{-5}).

(e) $8.9 \times 10^4 + 2.5 \times 10^5 = 0.89 \times 10^5 + 2.5 \times 10^5 = 3.4 \times 10^5$ (not 3.39×10^5).

---

5. Problem Solving (Section 1.7)

Problem solving is a skill that has to be learned gradually over a period of time. You can not learn this skill in a lecture or overnight. It takes practice—lots of practice—and the exact procedure you adopt will probably be unique to you. The point is to develop one that works for you; however, there are some suggested problem-solving procedures that can be followed.

(1)   *Say it in words.*

Read the problem carefully and analyze it. Write down the given data and what you are to find.

(2)   *Say it in pictures.*

Draw a diagram, if appropriate, as an aid in visualizing and analyzing the physical situation of the problem.

(3)   *Say it in equations.*

Determine which equation(s) are applicable to this situation and how they can be used to get from the information given to what is to be found.

(4)   *Simplify the equations.*

Simplify mathematical expressions as much as possible through algebraic manipulations before inserting actual numbers.

(5)   *Check the units.*

Check units before doing calculations.

(6)   Insert numbers and calculate; check significant figures.

Substitute given quantities into equation(s) and perform calculations. Report the result with proper units and the proper number of significant figures.

(7)   *Check the answer: is it reasonable?*

Consider whether the result is reasonable.

The details of these procedures can be found on pages 21 and 22 in the textbook.

Example 1.7:   Starting from city A, an airplane flies 250 miles east to city B, then 300 miles north to city C, and finally 700 miles west to city D. What is the distance from city A to city D?

Solution: Given: the distances and directions of each trip.

                    Find: the distance from city A to D.

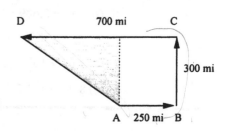

Following the problem statement, we draw a diagram. It is easy to see that the distance from A to D is the hypotenuse of the shaded right-angle triangle. The sides perpendicular to each other are 300 mi and (700 mi − 250 mi) = 450 mi.

To find the hypotenuse of a right-angle triangle, we use the Pythagorean theorem:

$c^2 = a^2 + b^2$, where a and b are the sides perpendicular to each other, and c is the hypotenuse

$$c = \sqrt{a^2 + b^2} = \sqrt{(300 \text{ mi})^2 + (450 \text{ mi})^2} = 541 \text{ mi}.$$

Obviously, the units, miles, are correct; the answer, 541, is reasonable; and the number of significant figures, 3, in the final result is the same as the least number of significant figures in 300 mi and 450 mi. These checks make us feel confident that we performed the right calculations.

Example 1.8:   The density of the metal aluminum is 2700 kg/m³. Find the mass of a solid aluminum cylinder of radius 10 cm and height 1.0 ft.

Solution: Given: the dimensions of the cylinder and the density of aluminum.

Find: the mass of the aluminum.

First, we find the volume of the cylinder. Because of the different units in the problem we first convert all cylinder dimensions to meters.

$$r = 10 \text{ cm} \frac{1 \text{ m}}{100 \text{ cm}} = 0.10 \text{ m}; \quad h = 1.0 \text{ ft} \frac{0.3048 \text{ m}}{1 \text{ ft}} = 0.3048 \text{ m}.$$

The volume of a cylinder is base area times height $= \pi r^2 h = \pi (0.10 \text{ m})^2 (0.3048 \text{ m}) = 9.58 \times 10^{-3} \text{ m}^3.$

Next, we find the mass of the cylinder.

Using the relation $\rho = \dfrac{m}{V}$ and multiplying by V on both sides we obtain $m = \rho V.$

Thus, $m = (2700 \text{ kg/m}^3)(9.58 \times 10^{-3} \text{ m}^3) = 26 \text{ kg}.$

In certain problems we may be interested only in the "ballpark" figure, that is, just an estimate of the result. This can be obtained by **order-of-magnitude calculations**. Approximations can be made by rounding off quantities to their nearest power-of-ten notation to make the calculations easier.

Example 1.9:   If each student's food intake is 3000 Calories per day, and a college has 6000 students, what is the approximate total food intake in a semester that last 3.5 months?

Solution: Given: each student's food intake per day, the number of days, and the number of students.

Find: the approximate total food intake.

The total food intake is the product of each student's food intake per day, the number of days, and the number of students.

Each student's food intake = 3000 Calories $\approx 10^3$ Calories/day.

The number of days = (3.5 months)(30 days/month) = 105 days $\approx 10^2$ days.

Number of students = 6000 $\approx 10^4.$

Thus, the total food intake is

$(10^3 \text{ Calories/day})(10^2 \text{ days})(10^4) = 10^9$ Calories.

Without the approximation, the result is

$(3000 \text{ Calories/day})(105 \text{ days})(6000) = 2 \times 10^9$ Calories

III. Mathematical Summary

Density	$\rho = \dfrac{m}{V} \left(\dfrac{\text{mass}}{\text{volume}}\right)$ (1.1)	Defines density in terms of mass and volume.

IV. Solutions of Selected Exercises and Paired Exercises

Keep in mind here and throughout the textbook that your answer to an exercise may differ slightly from that given at the back of the textbook or in this Study Guide because of rounding. See Problem-Solving Hint: The "Correct" Answer, in Chapter 1.

8. (a) Two *different* ounces are used. One is for volume measurement, and the other is for weight measurement.

(b) Again, two different pound units are used. Avoirdupois lb = 16 oz, and troy lb = 12 oz.

16. The dimension of the left side of the equation is   [L].

The dimension of the right side of the equation is $[L] + \dfrac{[L]}{[T]} \times [T] = [L] + [L].$

Thus, the dimension of the left side is equal to the dimension of the right side, and the equation is dimensionally correct.

22. From $x = \dfrac{gt^2}{2}$,   we have $g = \dfrac{2x}{t^2}$.

Thus, the units of g are the units of x divided by the units of t^2, that is, $\boxed{\text{m/s}^2}$.

27. Since $f = \dfrac{1}{2\pi} \sqrt{\dfrac{g}{L}}$, hertz $= \sqrt{\dfrac{\text{m/s}^2}{\text{m}}} = \boxed{\text{1/s or s}^{-1}}$.

28. (a) Because $F = ma$, newton $= (\text{kg})(\text{m/s}^2) = \boxed{\text{kg·m/s}^2}$.

(b) $\boxed{\text{Yes}}$. From $F = m\dfrac{v^2}{r}$, the units of force F are $(\text{kg}) \times \dfrac{(\text{m/s})^2}{\text{m}} = \text{kg} \cdot \text{m} / \text{s}^2$.

38. (a) Because 1 gal = 3.785 L < 4 L, or ½ gal < 2 L, ½ gal holds $\boxed{\text{less}}$.

(b) 0.5 gal = (0.5 gal) $\times \dfrac{3.785 \text{ L}}{1 \text{ gal}} = 1.89$ L.   2 L $-$ 1.89 L = 0.11 L. $\boxed{\text{2 L by 0.11 L more}}$.

42. $0.35 \text{ m/s} = (0.35 \text{ m/s}) \times \dfrac{1 \text{ mi}}{1609 \text{ m}} \times \dfrac{3600 \text{ s}}{1 \text{ h}} = 0.78 \text{ mi/h}$. Thus, a blood cell travels $\boxed{0.78 \text{ mi}}$ in 1 h.

45.   (a) $10 \text{ mi/h} = (10 \text{ mi/h}) \times \dfrac{1.609 \text{ km}}{1 \text{ mi}} = \boxed{16 \text{ km/h for each 10 mi/h}}$.

        (b) $70 \text{ mi/h} = (70 \text{ mi/h}) \times \dfrac{1.609 \text{ km}}{1 \text{ mi}} = \boxed{113 \text{ km/h}}$.

52.   (a) Using the $\dfrac{1 \text{ kg}}{1000 \text{ g}}$ and $\dfrac{100 \text{ cm}}{1 \text{ m}}$ conversion factors:

$$13.6 \text{ g/cm}^3 = (13.6 \text{ g/cm}^3) \times 1 \times 1 = (13.6 \text{ g/cm}^3) \times \dfrac{1 \text{ kg}}{1000 \text{ g}} \times \left(\dfrac{100 \text{ cm}}{1 \text{ m}}\right)^3 = \boxed{1.36 \times 10^4 \text{ kg/m}^3}.$$

The conversion factor $\dfrac{100 \text{ cm}}{1 \text{ m}}$ is cubed because we are converting cm^3 to m^3.

        (b) From $\rho = \dfrac{m}{V}$, we have $m = \rho V = (13.6 \text{ g/cm}^3)(0.250 \text{ L}) \times \dfrac{1000 \text{ cm}^3}{1 \text{ L}} = 3.40 \times 10^3 \text{ g} = \boxed{3.40 \text{ kg}}$.

58.   The last digit is estimated, so the smallest division is the third decimal place, that is, $\boxed{0.001 \text{ m or 1 mm}}$.

66.   From $V = a^3$, we have $a = \sqrt[3]{V} = \sqrt[3]{2.5 \times 10^2 \text{ cm}^3} = \boxed{6.3 \text{ cm}}$.

68.   (a) $\boxed{\text{Zero}}$, since 38 m has zero decimal place.

        (b) $46.9 \text{ m} + 5.72 \text{ m} - 38 \text{ m} = \boxed{15 \text{ m}}$.

74. $\rho = \dfrac{m}{V} = \dfrac{6.0 \times 10^{25} \text{ kg}}{1.1 \times 10^{21} \text{ m}^3} = \boxed{5.5 \times 10^3 \text{ kg/m}^3}$.

77.   (a) The percentage is $\dfrac{(18 \text{ g})(9 \text{ cal/g})}{310 \text{ cal}} = 0.52 = \boxed{52\%}$.

        (b) Total fat $= \dfrac{18 \text{ g}}{0.28} = \boxed{64 \text{ g}}$;   saturated fat $= \dfrac{7 \text{ g}}{0.35} = \boxed{20 \text{ g}}$.

80.   (a) From the sketch, the stadium is $\boxed{\text{south of west}}$, relative to your house.

        (b) Consider the right triangle at the bottom of the sketch. The two sides

perpendicular to each other are 500 m each. By the Pythagorean theorem,

$$d = \sqrt{(500 \text{ m})^2 + (500 \text{ m})^2} = \boxed{707 \text{ m}}.$$

500 m

1500 m   1000 m

d

87. By drawing a perpendicular line from the island to the shore, we see that the distance from the island to the shore is

$$d = x \tan 30° = (50 \text{ m} - x) \tan 40° = (50 \text{ m}) \tan 40° - x \tan 40°.$$

Solving, we obtain $x = \dfrac{(50 \text{ m}) \tan 40°}{\tan 30° + \tan 40°} = 29.6 \text{ m}.$

Therefore, $d = (29.6 \text{ m}) \tan 30° = \boxed{17 \text{ m}}.$

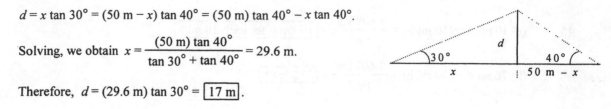

95. The volume of a cylinder is $V = AH$, where $A = \pi r^2$ is the area of the bottom of the cylinder, and H is the height of the cylinder.

Thus, $V = (\pi r^2)H = \pi(4.0 \text{ cm})^2(12 \text{ cm}) = 6.03 \times 10^2 \text{ cm}^3 = (6.03 \times 10^2 \text{ cm}^3) \times \dfrac{1 \text{ L}}{1000 \text{ cm}^3} = \boxed{0.60 \text{ L}}.$

99. (a) Since $d = (13 \text{ mi}) \tan 25°$, and $\tan 25° < 1$ ($\tan 45° = 1$),

d is $\boxed{\text{less than}}$ 13 mi.

(b) $d = (13 \text{ mi}) \tan 25° = \boxed{6.1 \text{ mi}}.$

V. Practice Quiz

1. The SI base units for length, mass, and time are

(a) meters, grams, seconds. (b) kilometers, kilograms, seconds.

(c) centimeters, kilograms, seconds. (d) meters, kilograms, seconds.

(e) kilometers, grams, seconds.

2. If v has units of m/s and t has units of s. What are the units of the quantity t/v?

(a) m (b) s^2/m (c) s/m (d) s/m^2 (e) s

3. Which one of the following has the same dimension as time?

(x is length, v is velocity, and a is acceleration)

(a) $\dfrac{x}{a}$ (b) $\sqrt{\dfrac{2x}{a}}$ (c) $\sqrt{\dfrac{v}{x}}$ (d) vx (e) xa

4. Which one of the following is *not* equivalent to 2.50 mi?

(a) 1.32×10^4 ft (b) 1.58×10^5 in. (c) 4.02×10^3 km (d) 4.02×10^5 cm (e) 4.40×10^3 yd

5.   When (3.51×10^4) is multiplied by (4.00×10^2), the product is which of the following expressed with the correct number of significant figures?

(a) 1.40×10^7 (b) 1.4×10^7 (c) 1×10^7 (d) 88   (e) 87.8

6.   The density of water is 1.0×10^3 kg/m^3. Find the mass of water needed to fill a 2.0-L soft-drink bottle.

(a) 0.020 kg   (b) 0.20 kg   (c) 2.0 kg   (d) 20 kg   (e) 200 kg

7.   The area of a room floor is 25 ft^2. How many square meters are on the floor?

(a) 7.6 m^2 (b) 2.3 m^2 (c) 82 m^2 (d) 2.6×10^2 m^2 (e) none of these

8.   An aluminum cube has a mass of 30 kg. What is the length of each side of the cube?
(The density of aluminum is 2.7×10^3 kg/m^3.)

(a) 0.011 m   (b) 0.11 m   (c) 1.4×10^{-6} m   (d) 0.22 m   (e) 0.022 m

9.   A person stands 35.0 m from a flagpole. With a protractor at eyelevel, he finds that the angle the top of the flagpole makes with the horizontal is 25.0°. How high is the flagpole? (The distance from his feet to his eyes is 1.70 m.)

(a) 14.8 m   (b) 16.3 m   (c) 16.5 m   (d) 18.0 m   (e) 75.1 m

10.   A rectangular garden measures 15 m long and 13.7 m wide. What is the length of a diagonal from one corner of the garden to the other?

(a) 29 m   (b) 1.0 m   (c) 18 m   (d) 4.1×10^2 m   (e) 20 m

11.   To go to a store from your house, you walk 500 m north, 300 m east, and then 700 m south. What is the straight-line distance from your house to the store?

(a) 1500 m   (b) 900 m   (c) 500 m   (d) 360 m   (e) 200 m

12.   A marine diesel engine, rotating through 1200 revolutions per minute, operates for 10 straight years. Estimate the total number of revolutions through which the engine rotates.

(a) about 10^{12} (b) about 10^9 (c) about 10^7 (d) about 10^5 (e) about 10^3

Answers to Practice Quiz:

1. d 2. b 3. b 4. c 5. a 6. c 7. b 8. d 9. d 10. e 11. d 12. b

CHAPTER 2

Kinematics: Description of Motion

I. Chapter Objectives

Upon completion of this chapter, you should be able to:

1. define distance and calculate speed, and explain what is meant by a scalar quantity.

2. define displacement and calculate velocity, and explain the difference between scalar and vector quantities.

3. explain the relationship between velocity and acceleration and perform graphical analyses of acceleration.

4. explain the kinematic equations of constant acceleration and apply them to physical situations.

5. use the kinetic equations to analyze free fall.

II. Chapter Summary and Discussion

1. Distance and Speed; Displacement and Velocity (Sections 2.1 – 2.2)

Motion is related to change of position. The length traveled in changing position may be expressed in terms of **distance**, the actual path length between two points. Distance is a scalar quantity, which has only a magnitude with no direction. The direct straight line pointing from the initial point to the final point is called **displacement** (change in position). Displacement measures only the change in position, not the details involved in the change in position. Displacement is a vector quantity, which has both magnitude and direction. In the figure shown, an object goes from point A to point C by following paths AB and BC. The distance traced is 3.0 m + 4.0 m = 7.0 m, and the displacement is 5.0 m in the direction of the arrow.

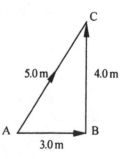

For motion in one dimension along the x-axis, the displacement between two points, x_1 and x_2, is simply the vector subtraction between x_1 and x_2: $\Delta x = x_2 - x_1$, where the Greek letter Δ (delta) is used to represent a change or difference in a quantity. For example, if an object moves from a point at $x_1 = 2.0$ m to another point at $x_2 = 4.0$ m, its displacement is $\Delta x = 4.0$ m $-$ 2.0 m $= +2.0$ m. The positive sign here indicates the direction of the displacement as along the positive *x*-axis; however, if the motion is reversed, then Δx = 2.0 m – 4.0 m = –2.0 m. (What is the meaning of the negative sign here?)

Example 2.1:   In a soccer game, a midfielder kicks the ball back 10 yards to a goalkeeper. The goalkeeper then kicks the ball straight up the field 50 yards to a forward. What is the distance traveled by the soccer ball? What is the displacement of the soccer ball?

Solution:

Sketch a diagram of the situation. For clarity, the arrows are laterally displaced.

It is obvious from the diagram that the soccer ball traveled 10 yards first and then 50 yards. Thus, the *distance traveled* is 10 yards + 50 yards = 60 yards.

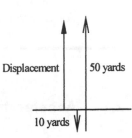

Displacement is the straight line from the initial position to the final position. The ball was displaced only 50 yards – 10 yards = 40 yards **straight up the field**.

Try to solve this problem without the diagram. You will find it is very difficult to do. That is why you are encouraged to try to draw a diagram to help solve a problem.

In a description of motion, the rate of change of position may be expressed in terms of speed and velocity.

Average speed is defined as the distance traveled divided by the time interval to travel that distance. $\bar{s} = \dfrac{d}{\Delta t}$, where $\bar{s}$ is average speed, d is distance traveled, and Δt is time interval (change in time).

Instantaneous speed is the speed at a particular time instant (Δt is infinitesimally small or close to zero). Because distance is a scalar quantity with no direction, so are average speed and instantaneous speed. Both values tell us only how fast objects are moving.

Average velocity is defined as *displacement* divided by the time interval, $\bar{v} = \dfrac{\Delta x}{\Delta t}$, where $\bar{v}$ is average velocity, Δx is displacement (change in position), and Δt is time interval. The sign of the displacement, positive or negative for one-dimensional motion, indicates the direction of displacement. **Instantaneous velocity, v,** is the velocity (magnitude and direction) at a particular instant of time (Δt is close to zero). Because displacement is a vector quantity, so are average velocity and instantaneous velocity. Both tell us not only how fast but in which directions objects are moving. The sign of velocity, positive or negative for one-dimensional motion, also indicates the direction of velocity. The SI units of speed and velocity are m/s.

Example 2.2: If the play described in Example 2.1 lasts 5.0 s, what is the average speed of the soccer ball? What is the average velocity of the soccer ball?

Solution:

Average speed:
$$\bar{s} = \frac{d}{\Delta t} = \frac{60 \text{ yd}}{5.0 \text{ s}} = 12 \text{ yd/s}.$$

Average velocity:
$$\bar{\mathbf{v}} = \frac{\Delta \mathbf{x}}{\Delta t} = \frac{40 \text{ yd straight up the field}}{5.0 \text{ s}} = 8.0 \text{ yd/s straight up the field}$$

2.   Acceleration (Section 2.3)

Acceleration is the rate of change of velocity with time. *Note*: It is the change in *velocity* (a vector), not speed (a scalar); hence, acceleration is also a vector.

Average acceleration is defined as the change in velocity divided by the time interval to make the change,

$$\bar{\mathbf{a}} = \frac{\Delta \mathbf{v}}{\Delta t} = \frac{\mathbf{v} - \mathbf{v}_0}{t - t_0}, \text{ where } \bar{\mathbf{a}} \text{ is average acceleration, } \Delta \mathbf{v} \text{ is change in velocity, and } \Delta t \text{ is time interval.}$$

Instantaneous acceleration is the acceleration at a particular instant of time (Δt is close to zero). Because velocity is a vector quantity, so are average acceleration and instantaneous acceleration. The SI units of acceleration are m/s/s or m/s^2. In many of the topics you are going to study, the motion will have a constant acceleration. If the acceleration is constant, then the average acceleration is equal to the instantaneous acceleration.

A common misconception about velocity and acceleration has to do with their directions. Because velocity has both magnitude and direction, a change in either magnitude (speed) or direction or both will result in a change in velocity, and therefore acceleration. We can accelerate objects either by speeding them up or slowing them down (change the magnitude of velocity) and/or by changing their direction of travel. We often call the gas pedal of a car an *accelerator*. Can we call the brake pedal an accelerator? Can we call the steering wheel an accelerator? The answers are yes to both questions. (Why?)

For motion in one dimension, when the velocity and acceleration of an object are in the same direction (they have the same directional signs), the velocity increases and the object speeds up (acceleration). When the velocity and acceleration are in opposite directions, the velocity decreases and the object slows down (deceleration). The Learn by Drawing on page 42 in the textbook graphically illustrates this point.

Example 2.3:   An object moving to the right has a decrease in velocity from 5.0 m/s to 1.0 m/s in 2.0 s. What is the average acceleration? What does your result mean?

Solution: Given: $v_0 = +5.0$ m/s, $v = +1.0$ m/s, $t = 2.0$ s.

Find: $\bar{a}$.

According to the definition of average acceleration,

$$\bar{a} = \frac{\Delta v}{\Delta t} = \frac{v - v_0}{t} = \frac{+1.0 \text{ m/s} - (+5.0 \text{ m/s})}{2.0 \text{ s}} = \frac{-4.0 \text{ m/s}}{2.0 \text{ s}} = -2.0 \text{ m/s}^2 .$$

The negative sign means that the acceleration is to the left, opposite the velocity (deceleration). The result means that the object *decreases* its velocity by 2.0 m/s every second or 2.0 m/s^2.

3.   Graphical Interpretation (Sections 2.2 - 2.3)

Graphical analysis is often helpful in understanding motion and its related quantities. In algebra, we learned that if $y = mx + b$, then m is the slope of the graph of y versus x. If we take $t_0 = 0$, then $\bar{a} = \frac{v - v_0}{t - t_0} = \frac{v - v_0}{t}$, or

$v = v_0 + \bar{a} t$. That is, the slope of a velocity-versus-time graph gives the average acceleration.

In general, on a position-versus-time graph, we can extract the average velocity by finding the slope of a line connecting two points. Instantaneous velocity is equal to the slope of a straight line tangent to the curve at a specific point. For a velocity-versus-time graph, the average acceleration is the slope of a straight line connecting two points, and instantaneous acceleration is the slope of a straight line tangent to the curve at a specific point. The area under the curve in a velocity-versus-time graph gives displacement, and the area under the curve in an acceleration-versus-time graph yields the change in velocity.

Example 2.4:   The graph represents the position of a particle as a function of time.

(a) What is the velocity at 1.0 s?

(b) What is the velocity at 2.5 s?

(c) What is the velocity at 4.0 s?

(d) What is the average velocity from 0 to 4.0 s?

(e) What is the average velocity for the 6.0-s interval?

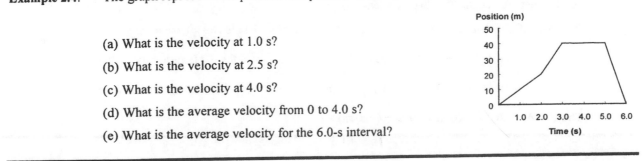

Solution:

(a) Velocity is the slope of the line. $\quad v = \dfrac{\Delta x}{\Delta t} = \dfrac{20 \text{ m} - 0 \text{ m}}{2.0 \text{ s} - 0 \text{ s}} = 10 \text{ m/s}.$

(b) Velocity is the slope of the line. $\quad v = \dfrac{\Delta x}{\Delta t} = \dfrac{40 \text{ m} - 20 \text{ m}}{3.0 \text{ s} - 2.0 \text{ s}} = 20 \text{ m/s}.$

(c) The slope of the line is zero, and so $v = 0$.

(d) $\bar{v} = \dfrac{\Delta x}{\Delta t} = \dfrac{40 \text{ m} - 0 \text{ m}}{4.0 \text{ s} - 0 \text{ s}} = 10 \text{ m/s}.$

(e) $\bar{v} = \dfrac{\Delta x}{\Delta t} = \dfrac{0 \text{ m} - 0 \text{ m}}{6.0 \text{ s} - 0 \text{ s}} = 0 \text{ m/s}.$

Example 2.5: The graph represents the velocity of a particle as a function of time.

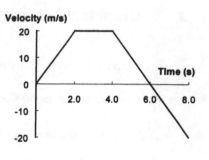

(a) What is the acceleration at 1.0 s?

(b) What is the acceleration at 3.0 s?

(c) What is the average acceleration between 0 and 5.0 s?

(d) What is the average acceleration for the 8.0-s interval?

(e) What is the displacement for the 8.0-s interval?

Solution:

(a) Acceleration is the slope of the line. $\quad a = \dfrac{\Delta v}{\Delta t} = \dfrac{20 \text{ m/s} - 0 \text{ m/s}}{2.0 \text{ s} - 0 \text{ s}} = 10 \text{ m/s}^2 .$

(b) The slope of the line is zero, so $a = 0$.

(c) $\bar{a} = \dfrac{\Delta v}{\Delta t} = \dfrac{10 \text{ m/s} - 0 \text{ m/s}}{5.0 \text{ s} - 0 \text{ s}} = 2.0 \text{ m/s}^2 .$

(d) $a = \dfrac{\Delta v}{\Delta t} = \dfrac{-20 \text{ m/s} - 0 \text{ m/s}}{8.0 \text{ s} - 0 \text{ s}} = -2.5 \text{ m/s}^2 .$

(e) The net area equals the displacement.

The area of a rectangle is length × width, and the area of a triangle is $\frac{1}{2}$ × base × height.

$$\Delta x_{0\text{-}2} = \tfrac{1}{2}(2.0 \text{ s} - 0 \text{ s})(20 \text{ m/s}) = 20 \text{ m}; \qquad \Delta x_{2\text{-}4} = (4.0 \text{ s} - 2.0 \text{ s})(20 \text{ m/s}) = 40 \text{ m};$$

$$\Delta x_{4\text{-}6} = \tfrac{1}{2}(6.0 \text{ s} - 4.0 \text{ s})(20 \text{ m/s}) = 20 \text{ m}; \qquad \Delta x_{6\text{-}8} = \tfrac{1}{2}(8.0 \text{ s} - 6.0 \text{ s})(-20 \text{ m/s}) = -20 \text{ m}.$$

Thus, $\quad \Delta x = 20 \text{ m} + 40 \text{ m} + 20 \text{ m} + (-20 \text{ m}) = 60 \text{ m}.$

---

4.   Kinematic Equations (Constant Acceleration) (Section 2.4)

Our discussion is restricted to **motions with constant accelerations**. In a motion with constant acceleration, the acceleration does not change with time or is a constant; however, the constant can be zero or a negative or a positive non-zero constant. Zero acceleration simply means that the velocity is a constant (no acceleration). For positive velocity, a negative acceleration means deceleration (speed decrease) and a positive acceleration means acceleration (speed increase). For negative velocity, a negative acceleration means acceleration (speed increase) and a positive acceleration means deceleration (speed decrease).

The symbols used in the kinematic equations are: v_0, initial velocity; v, final velocity; a, acceleration; $x - x_0$, displacement; t, time interval. Be aware that the terms *initial* and *final* are relative. The end of one event is always the beginning of another. There are three general equations and two algebraic combinations of these equations that provide calculation convenience.

$x = x_0 + \bar{v}t$ Final position = initial position + average velocity × times interval.

$\bar{v} = \dfrac{v + v_0}{2}$ Average velocity = $\dfrac{\text{final velocity} + \text{initial velocity}}{2}$.

$v = v_0 + at$ Final velocity = initial velocity + acceleration × time interval.

$x = x_0 + v_0 t + \frac{1}{2}at^2$ Final position = initial position + initial velocity × time interval

$+ \frac{1}{2} \times$ acceleration × time interval squared.

$v^2 = v_0^2 + 2a(x - x_0)$ Final velocity squared = initial velocity squared

$+ 2 \times$ acceleration × displacement.

Among the five equations listed, the last three can be used to solve the majority of kinematic problems. Which equation should you select in solving a particular problem? The equation you select must have the unknown quantity in it and everything else must be given, because you can solve only for one unknown in one equation.

Note that $(x - x_0)$, final position minus initial position, is the displacement of the object. This is explicitly expressed in $v^2 = v_0^2 + 2a(x - x_0)$. The equation $x = x_0 + v_0 t + \frac{1}{2}at^2$ can also be written as $(x - x_0) = v_0 t + \frac{1}{2}at^2$.

In many kinematic problems, we can set $x_0 = 0$ at the initial time. In other words, we can select a coordinate system so the object is at the origin when $t = 0$. The preceding equations can then be simplified, and the final position, x, will be the same as the displacement because $x - x_0 = x - 0 = x$.

Example 2.6:   An object starts from rest and accelerates with a constant acceleration of 5.0 m/s². Find its velocity and displacement at a time of 3.4 s.

Solution: Given: $v_0 = 0$ (starts from rest), $a = 5.0$ m/s^2, $t = 3.4$ s.

Find: v and $(x - x_0)$.

From $v = v_0 + at$, we have $v = 0 + (5.0$ m/s$^2)(3.4$ s$) = 17$ m/s.

Also $x - x_0 = v_0 t + \frac{1}{2} at^2 = (0)(3.4$ s$) + \frac{1}{2}(5.0$ m/s$^2)(3.4$ s$)^2 = 29$ m.

Both velocity and displacement are in the direction of the motion.

Example 2.7: An automobile accelerates uniformly from rest to 25 m/s while traveling 100 m. What is the acceleration of the automobile?

Solution: Given: $v_0 = 0$ (rest), $v = 25$ m/s, $(x - x_0) = 100$ m.

Find: a.

Since $v^2 = v_0^2 + 2a(x - x_0)$, $a = \dfrac{v^2 - v_0^2}{2(x - x_0)} = \dfrac{(25 \text{ m/s})^2 - (0)^2}{2(100 \text{ m})} = 3.1$ m/s^2.

Because a is positive, it is in the direction of the velocity or motion.

---

5. Free Fall (Section 2.5)

Objects in motion solely under the influence of gravity are said to be in **free fall**. A free fall does not necessarily mean a falling object. A vertically rising object is also said to be in free fall. The magnitude of **acceleration due to gravity** is often expressed by the symbol g. Near the surface of the Earth, the acceleration due to gravity is $g = 9.80$ m/s^2 (downward) and near the surface of the Moon, it is $g = 1.7$ m/s^2.

Note that g itself is a positive quantity, 9.80 m/s^2. If we use the upward direction as the positive reference direction, then we say the acceleration due to gravity is $-g = -9./80$ m/s^2 (downward 9.80 m/s^2); however, if we use the downward direction as the positive reference direction, then the acceleration due to gravity is $+g = +9./80$ m/s^2 (still downward 9.80 m/s^2).

Because free fall is in the vertical direction, and we often choose the upward direction as the $+y$ axis, we replace the x's with y's and a's with $-g$'s in the kinematic equation. The results are

$$y = y_0 + \bar{v}t, \quad \bar{v} = \frac{v + v_0}{2}, \quad v = v_0 - gt, \quad y = y_0 + v_0 t - \tfrac{1}{2}gt^2, \quad v^2 = v_0^2 - 2g(y - y_0), \text{ where } g = 9.80 \text{ m/s}^2.$$

In many free-fall situations, we can take $y_0 = 0$ to simplify the application of the preceding equations. Also note that $(y - y_0)$ is the displacement of the object.

Example 2.8: A ball is thrown upward with an initial velocity near the surface of the Earth. When it reaches the highest point

    (a) its velocity is zero, and its acceleration is nonzero.

    (b) its velocity is zero, and its acceleration is zero.

    (c) its velocity is nonzero, and its acceleration is zero.

    (d) its velocity is nonzero, and its acceleration is nonzero.

Solution:

The answer is (a), not (b), as you might think. The velocity has to change its direction at the highest point (goes from positive to negative) and so it is zero; however, the acceleration is not zero there. The acceleration is a constant 9.80 m/s^2 downward, independent of velocity. Stop and think, what if both the velocity and acceleration were zero at the highest point? Would the ball fall down from the highest point?

Example 2.9: A ball is thrown upward with an initial velocity of 10.0 m/s from the top of a 50.0 m tall building.

    (a) With what velocity will the ball strike the ground?

    (b) How long does it take the ball to strike the ground?

Solution: Given: $(y - y_o) = -50.0$ m (displacement), $v_o = +10.0$ m/s.

              Find: (a) v (b) t.

$(y - y_o)$, the difference between the final position and the initial position, is, by definition, displacement, not distance. When the ball strikes the ground, it will have been displaced -50.0 m, or 50 m below the launch point.

$y - y_o = -50.0$ m

(a) $v^2 = v_o^2 - 2g(y - y_o) = (+10.0 \text{ m/s})^2 - 2(9.80 \text{ m/s}^2)(-50.0 \text{ m})$

      $= 1.08 \times 10^3$ m^2/s^2.   So $v = \sqrt{1.08 \times 10^3 \text{ m}^2 / \text{s}^2} = \pm 32.9$ m / s.

The positive answer is discarded, since the ball is falling when it lands (moving downward).

Therefore, $v = -32.9$ m/s.

(b) From $v = v_o - gt$, we have

$$t = \frac{v_o - v}{g} = \frac{(+10.0 \text{ m/s} - (-32.9 \text{ m/s})}{9.80 \text{ m/s}^2} = \frac{42.9 \text{ m/s}}{9.80 \text{ m/s}^2} = 4.38 \text{ s}.$$

Try to solve this problem without using the overall displacement concept. You could break it into two phases. First, you would have to find out how high the ball goes, then second, determine the velocity when it strikes the ground, and the total time it is in the air.

III.   Mathematical Summary

Average speed	$\bar{s} = \dfrac{d}{t}$ (2.1)	Defines average speed.
Average velocity	$\bar{v} = \dfrac{\Delta x}{\Delta t}$ or $x = x_o + \bar{v}t$ (2.3)	Defines average velocity or expresses position in terms of average velocity and time interval
Average acceleration	$\bar{a} = \dfrac{\Delta v}{\Delta t}$ (2.5)	Defines average acceleration.
Kinematic equation	$\bar{v} = \dfrac{v + v_o}{2}$ (2.9)	Defines average velocity for motion with constant acceleration.
Kinematic equation	$v = v_o + at$ (2.8)	Relates final velocity with initial velocity, acceleration, and time (constant acceleration only).
Kinematic equation	$x = x_o + v_o t + \frac{1}{2}at^2$ (2.11)	Relates displacement with initial velocity, acceleration, and time (constant acceleration only).
Kinematic equation	$v^2 = v_o^2 + 2a(x - x_o)$ (2.12)	Relates final velocity with initial velocity, acceleration, and displacement (constant acceleration only).
Equation (free fall)	$v = v_o - gt$ (2.8')	Relates final velocity with initial velocity, acceleration, and time.
Equation (free fall)	$y = y_o + v_o t - \frac{1}{2}gt^2$ (2.11')	Relates displacement with initial velocity, acceleration, and time.
Equation (free fall)	$v^2 = v_o^2 - 2g(y - y_o)$ (2.12')	Relates final velocity with initial velocity, acceleration, and displacement.

IV.   Solutions of Selected Exercises and Paired Exercises

10.   Displacement is the change in position.

Thus, the magnitude of the displacement for half a lap is $\boxed{300 \text{ m}}$.

For a full lap (the car returns to its starting position), the displacement is $\boxed{\text{zero}}$.

14.   (a) First trip: $\bar{s} = \dfrac{d}{\Delta t} = \dfrac{150 \text{ km}}{2.5 \text{ h}} = \boxed{60 \text{ km/h}}$.

Return trip: $\bar{s} = \dfrac{150 \text{ km}}{2.0 \text{ h}} = \boxed{75 \text{ km/h}}$.

(b) Total trip: $\bar{s} = \dfrac{150 \text{ km} + 150 \text{ km}}{2.5 \text{ h} + 2.0 \text{ h}} = \boxed{67 \text{ km/h}}$.

17.   (a) The magnitude of the displacement is $\boxed{\text{between 40 m and 60 m}}$, as any

side of a triangle cannot be greater than the sum of the other two sides. In

this case, looking at the triangle shown, the two sides perpendicular to each

other are 20 m and 40 m, respectively. The magnitude of the displacement is

the hypotenuse of the right triangle, so it cannot be smaller than the longer of

the sides perpendicular to each other.

(b) $d = \sqrt{(40\text{ m})^2 + (50\text{m} - 30\text{ m})^2} = \boxed{45\text{ m}}$. $\theta = \tan^{-1}\left(\dfrac{50\text{ m} - 30\text{ m}}{40\text{ m}}\right) = \boxed{27° \text{ west of north}}$.

18.   (a) $\bar{s} = \dfrac{d}{\Delta t} = = \dfrac{2(7.1\text{ m})}{2.4\text{ s}} = \boxed{5.9\text{ m/s}}$.

(b) Because the ball is caught at the initial height, the displacement is zero.

Thus, the average velocity is $\boxed{\text{zero}}$.

22.   (a) $\bar{v} = \dfrac{\Delta x}{\Delta t}$,

$\bar{v}_{AB} = \dfrac{1.0\text{ m} - 1.0\text{ m}}{1.0\text{ s} - 0} = \boxed{0}$; $\bar{v}_{BC} = \dfrac{7.0\text{ m} - 1.0\text{ m}}{3.0\text{ s} - 1.0\text{ s}} = \boxed{3.0\text{ m/s}}$;

$\bar{v}_{CD} = \dfrac{9.0\text{ m} - 7.0\text{ m}}{4.5\text{ s} - 3.0\text{ s}} = \boxed{1.3\text{ m/s}}$; $\bar{v}_{DE} = \dfrac{7.0\text{ m} - 9.0\text{ m}}{6.0\text{ s} - 4.5\text{ s}} = \boxed{-1.3\text{ m/s}}$;

$\bar{v}_{EF} = \dfrac{2.0\text{ m} - 7.0\text{ m}}{9.0\text{ s} - 6.0\text{ s}} = \boxed{-1.7\text{ m/s}}$; $\bar{v}_{FG} = \dfrac{2.0\text{ m} - 2.0\text{ m}}{11.0\text{ s} - 9.0\text{ s}} = \boxed{0}$;

$\bar{v}_{BG} = \dfrac{2.0\text{ m} - 1.0\text{ m}}{11.0\text{ s} - 1.0\text{ s}} = \boxed{0.10\text{ m/s}}$.

(b) $\boxed{\text{The motion of BC, CD, and DE are not uniform}}$, since they are not straight lines.

(c) The object changes its direction of motion at point D, so it has to stop momentarily, and $v = \boxed{0}$.

28.   To the runner on the right, the runner on the left is running at a velocity of

$+4.50\text{ m/s} - (-3.50\text{ m/s}) = +8.00\text{ m/s}$.

From $\bar{v} = \dfrac{\Delta x}{\Delta t}$, we have $\Delta t = \dfrac{\Delta x}{\bar{v}} = \dfrac{100\text{ m}}{8.00\text{ m/s}} = \boxed{12.5\text{ s}}$.

They meet at $(4.50\text{ m/s})(12.5\text{ s}) = \boxed{56.3\text{ m from the initial position of the runner on left}}$.

30.   (d). Any change in either magnitude or direction results in a change in velocity. The brakes and gearshift

change the magnitude, and the steering wheel changes the direction.

38. $$60 \text{ mi/h} = (60 \text{ mi/h}) \times \frac{1609 \text{ m}}{1 \text{ mi}} \times \frac{1 \text{ h}}{3600 \text{ s}} = 26.8 \text{ m/s}.$$

$$\bar{a} = \frac{\Delta v}{\Delta t} = \frac{26.8 \text{ m/s} - 0}{3.9 \text{ s}} = \boxed{6.9 \text{ m/s}^2}$$

45. $$72 \text{ km/h} = (72 \text{ km/h}) \times \frac{1000 \text{ m}}{1 \text{ km}} \times \frac{1 \text{ h}}{3600 \text{ s}} = 20 \text{ m/s}.$$

During deceleration, $\quad \Delta t_1 = \dfrac{\Delta v}{\bar{a}} = \dfrac{0 - 20 \text{ m/s}}{-1.0 \text{ m/s}^2} = 20 \text{ s};$

$$\Delta x_1 = \bar{v}_1 \Delta t_1 = \frac{20 \text{ m/s} + 0}{2} (20 \text{ s}) = 200 \text{ m}.$$

It would have taken the train $\dfrac{200 \text{ m}}{20 \text{ m/s}} = 10 \text{ s}$ to travel 200 m,

it lost only 20 s – 10 s = 10 s during deceleration.

During acceleration, $\quad \Delta t_2 = \dfrac{20 \text{ m/s} - 0}{0.50 \text{ m/s}^2} = 40 \text{ s};$

$$\Delta x_2 = \frac{0 + 20 \text{ m/s}}{2} (40 \text{ s}) = 400 \text{ m}.$$

It would have taken the train $\dfrac{400 \text{ m}}{20 \text{ m/s}} = 20 \text{ s}$ to travel 400 m, so it lost only 40 s – 20 s = 20 s during

acceleration. Therefore, the train lost 2 min + 10 s + 20 s = $\boxed{150 \text{ s}}$ in stopping at the station.

52. Given: $v_o = 0$, $\quad a = 2.0 \text{ m/s}^2$, $\quad t = 5.00 \text{ s}$. Find: v and x. (Take $x_o = 0$.)

(a) $v = v_o + at = 0 + (2.0 \text{ m/s}^2)(5.0 \text{ s}) = \boxed{10 \text{ m/s}}$.

(b) $x = x_o + v_o t + \frac{1}{2} at^2 = 0 + 0(5.00 \text{ s}) + \frac{1}{2}(2.0 \text{ m/s}^2)(5.0 \text{ s})^2 = \boxed{25 \text{ m}}$.

56. Given: $v_o = 0$, $\quad v = 560 \text{ km/h} = 155.6 \text{ m/s}$, $\quad x = 400 \text{ m}$ (Take $x_o = 0$.).

Find: t and a.

(a) From $x = x_o + \bar{v}t = 0 + \bar{v}t = \dfrac{v_o + v}{2} t$, $\quad$ so $\quad t = \dfrac{2x}{v_o + v} = \dfrac{2(400 \text{ m})}{0 + 155.6 \text{ m/s}} = \boxed{5.14 \text{ s}}$.

(b) Since $v = v_o + at$, $a = \dfrac{v - v_o}{t} = \dfrac{155.6 \text{ m/s} - 0}{5.14 \text{ s}} = \boxed{30.3 \text{ s}}$.

59. (a) $\boxed{\text{The object will travel in the } +x\text{-direction and then reverse its direction}}$. This is because the object has

initial velocity in the +x-direction and it takes time for the object to decelerate and stop, then reverse

direction. We take $x_o = 0$.

Given: $v_o = 40 \text{ m/s}$, $\quad a = -3.5 \text{ m/s}^2$, $\quad x = 0$ ("returns to the origin"). Find: t and v.

(b) Since $x = x_o + v_o t + \frac{1}{2}at^2$, $0 = 0 + (40 \text{ m/s})t + \frac{1}{2}(-3.5 \text{ m/s}^2)t^2$.

Reduce to quadratic equation: $1.75t^2 - 40t = 0$.

Solve for $t = 0$ or 22.9 s.

The $t = 0$ answer corresponds to the initial time, so the answer is $t = \boxed{23 \text{ s}}$.

(c) $v = v_o + at = 40 \text{ m/s} + (-3.5 \text{ m/s}^2)(22.9 \text{ s}) = \boxed{-40 \text{ m/s}}$.

The negative sign means the object is traveling in the $-x$ direction.

60.   Given: $v_o = 330$ m/s, $v = 0$, $x = 30$ cm $= 0.30$ m. (Take $x_o = 0$.)   Find: a.

From $v^2 = v_o^2 + 2a(x - x_o)$, we have $a = \dfrac{v^2 - v_o^2}{2x} = \dfrac{(0)^2 - (330 \text{ m/s})^2}{2(0.30 \text{ m})} = -\boxed{1.8 \times 10^5 \text{ m/s}^2}$.

The negative sign here indicates that the direction of the acceleration vector is opposite the velocity vector.

64. $40 \text{ km/h} = (40 \text{ km/h}) \times \dfrac{1000 \text{ m}}{1 \text{ km}} \times \dfrac{1 \text{ h}}{3600 \text{ s}} = 11.11 \text{ m/s}$.

During reaction, the car travels a distance of $d = (11.11 \text{ m/s})(0.25 \text{ s}) = 2.78$ m,

so the car really has only $13 \text{ m} - 2.78 \text{ m} = 10.2$ m to come to rest.

Let's calculate the stopping distance of the car. We take $x_o = 0$.

Given: $v_o = 11.1$ m/s, $v = 0$, $a = -8.0$ m/s^2.   Find: x.

From $v^2 = v_o^2 + 2a(x - x_o)$, we have $x = \dfrac{v^2 - v_o^2}{2a} = \dfrac{0 - (11.1 \text{ m/s})^2}{2(-8.0 \text{ m/s}^2)} = 7.70$ m,

so it takes the car only $2.78 \text{ m} + 7.70 \text{ m} = \boxed{10.5 \text{ m} < 13 \text{ m}}$ to stop.

$\boxed{\text{Yes}}$, the car will stop before hitting the child.

68.   (a) We take $x_o = 0$. From $v^2 = v_o^2 + 2a(x - x_o)$, we have $x = \dfrac{v^2 - v_o^2}{2a} = \dfrac{0^2 - v_o^2}{2a} = -\dfrac{v_o^2}{2a}$,

so x is proportional to v_o^2. If v_o doubles, then x becomes 4 times as large.

The answer is then $\boxed{4x}$.

(b) $\dfrac{x_2}{x_1} = \dfrac{v_{2o}^2}{v_{1o}^2} = \dfrac{60^2}{40^2} = 2.25$,

so $x_2 = 2.25x_1 = 2.25\,(3.00 \text{ m}) = \boxed{6.75 \text{ m}}$.

74.   (c). It accelerates at 9.80 m/s^2, so it increases its speed by 9.80 m/s in each second.

79.   (a) We take $y_o = 0$. $y = y_o + v_o t - \frac{1}{2}gt^2 = -\frac{1}{2}gt^2$, so y is proportional to the time squared.

So twice the time means $\boxed{4 \text{ times}}$ the height.

Given: $v_o = 0$, $t = 1.80$ s.   Find: y_A and y_B.

(b) $y_A = -\frac{1}{2}(9.80 \text{ m/s}^2)(1.80 \text{ s})^2 = -15.9$ m,

so the height of cliff A above the water is $\boxed{15.9 \text{ m}}$.

$y_B = \dfrac{y_A}{4} = \dfrac{15.9 \text{ m}}{4} = \boxed{4.0 \text{ m}}$.

82.   Given: $v_o = 15$ m/s, $v = 0$ (maximum height).   Find: y. (Take $y_o = 0$.)

From $v^2 = v_o^2 - 2g(y - y_o)$, we have $y = \dfrac{v_o^2 - v^2}{2g} = \dfrac{(15 \text{ m/s})^2 - (0)^2}{2(9.80 \text{ m/s}^2)} = \boxed{11 \text{ m}}$.

84.   (a) Given: $v_o = 21$ m/s, $t = 3.0$ s.   Find: y. (Take $y_o = 0$.)

$y = y_o + v_o t - \frac{1}{2}gt^2 = 0 + (21 \text{ m/s})(3.0 \text{ s}) - \frac{1}{2}(9.80 \text{ m/s}^2)(3.0 \text{ s})^2 = \boxed{19 \text{ m}}$.

(b) $12 \text{ m} = (21 \text{ m/s})t - \frac{1}{2}(9.80 \text{ m/s}^2)t^2$,   or $4.90t^2 - 21t + 12 = 0$.

Solve the quadratic equation for $t = \boxed{0.68 \text{ s (on the way up) or 3.6 s (on the way down)}}$.

87.   We take $y_o = 0$.

(a) Given: $v_o = -14$ m/s, $t = 2.00$ s.   Find: y.

$y = y_o + v_o t - \frac{1}{2}gt^2 = 0 + (-14 \text{ m/s})(2.00 \text{ s}) - \frac{1}{2}(9.80 \text{ m/s}^2)(2.00 \text{ s})^2 = \boxed{-48 \text{ m}}$.

(b) Given: $v_o = -14$ m/s, $y = -65.0$ m.   Find: v.

$v^2 = v_o^2 - 2g(y - y_o) = (-14 \text{ m/s})^2 - 2(9.80 \text{ m/s}^2)(-65.0 \text{ m}) = 1.47 \times 10^3 \text{ m}^2/\text{s}^2$,

so $v = -\sqrt{1.47 \times 10^3 \text{ m}^2/\text{s}^2} = -38 \text{ m/s} = \boxed{38 \text{ m/s downward}}$.

91.   We take $y_o = 0$.

(a) When the ball rebounds, it is in free fall with an initial upward velocity. At the maximum height, the velocity is zero.

From $v^2 = v_o^2 - 2g(y - y_o)$, we have $y = \dfrac{v_o^2 - v^2}{2g}$,   so $y_{max} = \dfrac{v_o^2}{2g}$.

Therefore, the height depends on the initial velocity squared.

$95\% = 0.95$ and $0.95^2 = 0.90 < 0.95$.

The ball will bounce $\boxed{\text{less than}}$ 95% of the initial height.

(b) First, calculate the speed just before impact.

Given: $v_0 = 0$, $y = -4.00$ m. Find: v.

$$v^2 = v_0^2 - 2g(y - y_0) = 0^2 - 2(9.80 \text{ m/s}^2)(-4.00 \text{ m}) = 78.4 \text{ m}^2/\text{s}^2,$$

so $v = -\sqrt{78.4 \text{ m}^2/\text{s}^2} = -8.85$ m/s.

Therefore, the speed right after rebound is $0.950(8.85 \text{ m/s}) = 8.41$ m/s.

Now consider the rising motion.

Given: $v_0 = 8.41$ m/s, $v = 0$ (max height). Find: y.

From $v^2 = v_0^2 - 2g(y - y_0)$, we have $y = \dfrac{v_0^2 - v^2}{2g} = \dfrac{(8.41 \text{ m/s})^2 - 0^2}{2(9.80 \text{ m/s}^2)} = \boxed{3.61 \text{ m}}$.

94. (a) Given: $v_0 = 12.50$ m/s (ascending), $y = -60.0$ m (Take $y_0 = 0$.). Find: t.

From $y = y_0 + v_0 t - \frac{1}{2}gt^2$, we have -60.0 m $= 0 + (12.50 \text{ m/s})t - (4.90 \text{ m/s}^2)t^2$.

Reduce to a quadratic equation: $4.90t^2 - 12.50t - 60.0 = 0$.

Solve for $t = \boxed{5.00 \text{ s}}$ or -2.45 s, which is physically meaningless.

(b) $v = v_0 - gt = 12.50$ m/s $- (9.80 \text{ m/s}^2)(5.00 \text{ s}) = -36.5$ m/s $= \boxed{36.5 \text{ m/s}}$ downward.

111. (a) The speed of sound is considered here because it takes time for the sound of the stone hitting water to travel from the bottom of the well to the person.

(b) The time for the stone and sound to travel is 3.65 s $- 0.250$ s $= 3.40$ s. Assume the depth of the well is d, and it takes t_1 for the stone to reach the bottom and t_2 for sound to travel to the top. We take $y_0 = 0$.

For the stone: From $d = y = y_0 + v_0 t - \frac{1}{2}gt^2 = -\frac{1}{2}gt^2$, we have $t_1 = \sqrt{\dfrac{2d}{g}}$.

For sound: $t_2 = \dfrac{d}{v_s}$, so 3.40 s $= t_1 + t_2 = \sqrt{\dfrac{2d}{9.80 \text{ m/s}^2}} + \dfrac{d}{340 \text{ m/s}}$.

Simplify to a quadratic equation: $d^2 - (2.590 \times 10^4)d + 1.336 \times 10^6 = 0$.

Solve for $d = \boxed{51.5 \text{ m}}$. (Using 4 significant figures.)

V. Practice Quiz

1. If you run a full lap around a circular track of radius 25 m in 100 s, the magnitude of your average velocity is

(a) zero. (b) 0.20 m/s. (c) 0.50 m/s. (d) 1.0 m/s. (e) 3.14 m/s.

2.	An object moving along the +x-axis experiences an acceleration of +5.0 m/s². This means the object is

	(a) traveling 5.0 m in every second.

	(b) traveling at 5.0 m/s in every second.

	(c) changing its velocity by 5.0 m/s.

	(d) increasing its velocity by 5.0 m/s in every second.

3.	A car starts from rest and travels 100 m in 5.0 s. What is the magnitude of the constant acceleration?

	(a) zero (b) 5.0 m/s² (c) 8.0 m/s² (d) 10 m/s² (e) 40 m/s²

4.	An object is thrown straight up. When it is at the highest point

	(a) both its velocity and acceleration are zero.

	(b) neither its velocity nor its acceleration is zero.

	(c) its velocity is zero, and its acceleration is not zero.

	(d) its velocity is not zero, and its acceleration is zero.

5.	Human reaction time is usually greater than 0.10 s. If your lab partner holds a ruler between your fingers and releases it without warning, how far can you expect the ruler to fall before you catch it?

	(a) at least 3.0 cm (b) at least 4.9 cm (c) at least 6.8 cm (d) at least 9.8 cm (e) at least 11.0 cm

6.	Which one of the following quantities is an example of a vector?

	(a) distance (b) acceleration (c) speed (d) mass

7.	A ball is thrown vertically upward with a speed v. An identical second ball is thrown upward with a speed $2v$ (twice as fast). What is the ratio of the maximum height of the second ball to that of the first ball? (How many times higher does the second ball go than the first ball?)

	(a) 4:1 (b) 2:1 (c) 1.7:1 (d) 1.4:1 (e) 1:1

8.	A car starts from rest and accelerates for 4.0 m/s² for 5.0 s, then maintains that velocity for 10 s and then decelerates at the rate of 2.0 m/s² for 4.0 s. What is the final speed of the car?

	(a) 20 m/s (b) 16 m/s (c) 12 m/s (d) 10 m/s (e) 8.0 m/s

9.	An object moves 5.0 m north and then 3.0 m east. Find both the distance traveled and the magnitude of the displacement.

	(a) 8.0 m; 5.8 m (b) 5.8 m; 8.0 m (c) 8.0 m; 4.0 m (d) 4.0 m; 8.0 m (e) 5.8 m, 34 m

10.	A car with a speed of 25.0 m/s brakes to a stop. If the maximum deceleration of the car is 10.0 m/s², what is the minimum stopping distance?

	(a) 0.032 m (b) 0.80 m (c) 1.3 m (d) 31 m (e) 6.3×10^2 m

11.   An object moves along the +x-axis. At $x = 10$ m, its speed is 5.0 m/s. At 4.0 s later, the object is at $x = 70$ m. What is its acceleration?

(a) 1.0 m/s^2 (b) 5.0 m/s^2 (c) 10 m/s^2 (d) 15 m/s^2 (e) 20 m/s^2

12.   A stone is thrown vertically upward at an initial speed of 10 m/s from a height of 20 m above the ground. How long is the stone in the air before it hits the ground?

(a) 1.2 s   (b) 2.0 s   (c) 3.3 s   (d) 4.5 s   (e) 10 s

Answers to Practice Quiz:

CHAPTER 3

Motion in Two Dimensions

I. Chapter Objectives

Upon completion of this chapter, you should be able to:

1. analyze motion in terms of its components and apply the kinematic equations to components of motion.

2. learn vector notation, add and subtract vectors graphically and analytically, and use vectors to describe motion in two dimensions.

3. determine relative velocities through vector addition and subtraction.

4. analyze projectile motion to find position, time of flight, and range.

II. Chapter Summary and Discussion

1. Components of Motion (Section 3.1)

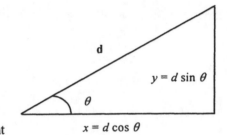

Motion in two dimensions, or curvilinear motion, is motion in which an object moves in a plane that can be described by a rectangular coordinate system. When such motion is analyzed, quantities are usually resolved into rectangular **components**. The diagram shows the displacement vector being resolved into $x = d \cos \theta$ and $y = d \sin \theta$, the rectangular coordinates. Similarly, velocity and acceleration vectors, **v** and **a**, are resolved into $v_x = v \cos\theta$, $v_y = v \sin \theta$, and $a_x = a \cos \theta$, $a_y = a \sin \theta$, their horizontal and vertical components, respectively.

Note: The angle θ used in the preceding calculations is the angle relative to the x-axis.

Once the displacement, velocity, and acceleration vectors are resolved into their respective components, we can apply the kinematic equations from Chapter 2 to the motion in the x- and y-directions. For example:

$$v_x = v_{xo} + a_x t, \quad x = x_o + v_{xo} t + \tfrac{1}{2} a_x t^2,$$

$$v_y = v_{yo} + a_y t, \quad y = y_o + v_{yo} t + \tfrac{1}{2} a_y t^2, \quad \text{etc.}$$

The key to success in solving two-dimensional motion is to resolve the motion into components. Remember to treat the components as independent, i.e., a_x having nothing to do with a_y, and so forth; however, the time in all the equations is the same, providing a common link. Always think about resolving vectors into components when working problems in two dimensions.

Example 3.1: An airplane is moving at 250 mi/h in a direction 35° north of east. Find the components of the plane's velocity in the eastward and northward directions.

Solution: Given: $\mathbf{v} = 250$ mi/h in a direction 35° north of east,

or $v = 250$ mi/h and $\theta = 35°$.

Find: v_E and v_N.

$v_E = v \cos \theta = (250 \text{ mi/h}) \cos 35° = 205$ mi/h;

$v_N = v \sin \theta = (250 \text{ mi/h}) \sin 35° = 143$ mi/h.

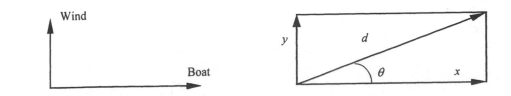

Example 3.2: A boat is traveling with a speed of 5.0 m/s in a straight path on a still lake. Suddenly, a steady wind pushes the boat perpendicular to its straight-line path with a speed of 3.0 m/s for 5.0 s. Relative to its position just when the wind started to blow, where is the boat at the end of this time?

Solution: Given: $v_{xo} = 5.0$ m/s, $a_x = 0$, $v_{yo} = 3.0$ m/s, $a_x = 0$, $t = 5.0$ s.

Find: x and y.

Both motions are motions with constant velocity (zero acceleration). Choose the straight path of the boat as the x-axis and the direction of wind as the y-axis. Take both $x_o = 0$ and $y_o = 0$.

$x = x_o + v_{xo} t + \tfrac{1}{2} a_x t^2 = 0 + (5.0 \text{ m/s})(5.0 \text{ s}) + 0 = 25$ m,

$y = y_o + v_{xo} t + \tfrac{1}{2} a_x t^2 = 0 + (3.0 \text{ m/s})(5.0 \text{ s}) + 0 = 15$ m.

Or $d = \sqrt{x^2 + y^2} = \sqrt{(25 \text{ m})^2 + (15 \text{ m})^2} = 29$ m,

and $\theta = \tan^{-1} \dfrac{y}{x} = \tan^{-1} \dfrac{15 \text{ m}}{25 \text{ m}} = \tan^{-1} 0.60 = 31°$.

---

2.   Vector Addition and Subtraction (Section 3.2)

Vector addition can be done geometrically with the triangle method or the parallelogram method for two vectors and with the polygon method for more than two vectors. **Vector subtraction** is a special case of vector addition because **A** − **B** = **A** + (−**B**), and a negative vector is defined as a vector having the same magnitude but opposite direction of the positive vector. For example, the negative vector of a velocity vector at 45 m/s north is simply a vector at 45 m/s south. A convenient and consistent scale must be used for adding or subtracting vectors geometrically.

Example 3.3:   Two vectors **A** and **B** are given. Show

(a) **A** + **B** with the triangle method.

(b) **A** + **B** with the parallelogram method.

(c) **A** − **B** with the triangle method.

(d) **A** − **B** with the parallelogram method.

Solution: (a)   (b)

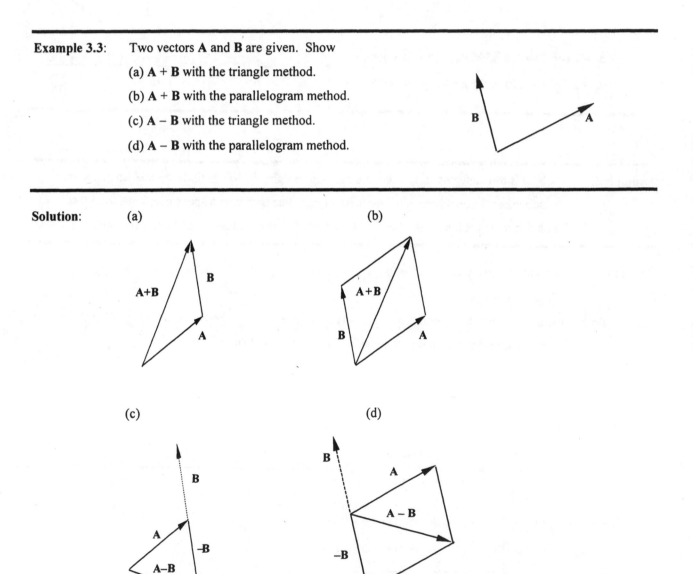

(c)   (d)

Vector addition is conveniently done by the **analytical component method**. The recommended procedure is as follows:

(1)   Resolve the vectors to be added into their x- and y-components. Include directional signs (positive or negative) in the components.

(2)   Add, algebraically, all the x-components together and all the y-components together to get the x- and y-components of the resultant vector, respectively.

(3)   Express the resultant vector using   (a) the component form, e.g., $\mathbf{A} = A_x\,\hat{\mathbf{x}} + A_y\,\hat{\mathbf{y}}$, or

(b) the magnitude-angle form, e.g., $A = \sqrt{A_x^2 + A_y^2}$,

$$\theta = \tan^{-1}\frac{A_y}{A_x}\text{ (relative to } x\text{-axis)}.$$

A detailed treatment of this procedure can be found on pages 75 to 76 in the textbook.

Example 3.4:   Use the analytical component method to find the resultant velocity of the following two velocities:

(i) $\mathbf{v}_1 = 35$ m/s 30° north of east;

(ii) $\mathbf{v}_2 = 55$ m/s 45° north of west.

Solution:

(1)   Resolve the vectors to be added into their x- and y-components.

$v_{1x} = v_1 \cos 30° = (35$ m/s$) \cos 30° = 30.3$ m/s;

$v_{1y} = (35$ m/s$) \sin 30° = 17.5$ m/s.

$v_{2x} = -v_2 \cos 45° = -(55$ m/s$) \cos 45° = -38.9$ m/s, ($-x$ direction)

(Why is the x-component of $\mathbf{v}_2$ negative?)

$v_{2y} = (55$ m/s$) \sin 45° = 38.9$ m/s.

(2)   Add components.

$v_x = v_{1x} + v_{2x} = 30.3$ m/s $+ (-38.9$ m/s$) = -8.6$ m/s,

$v_y = v_{1y} + v_{2y} = 17.5$ m/s $+ 38.9$ m/s $= 56.4$ m/s.

(3)   Express the resultant vector.

First, we draw the resultant velocity vector based on the components obtained in the previous procedure. We know that the x-component is -8.6 m/s, and the y-component is 56.4 m/s.

In component form: $\mathbf{v} = \mathbf{v}_1 + \mathbf{v}_2 = -8.6$ m/s $\hat{\mathbf{x}} + 56$ m/s $\hat{\mathbf{y}}$;

In magnitude-angle form: $v = \sqrt{v_x^2 + v_y^2} = \sqrt{(-8.6 \text{ m/s})^2 + (56.4 \text{ m/s})^2} = 57$ m/s,

and $\theta = \tan^{-1}\dfrac{v_y}{v_x} = \tan^{-1}\dfrac{56.4 \text{ m/s}}{-8.6 \text{ m/s}} = 81°$ north of west.

Note: Once you have the components for the resultant [at the end of step 2], you need to draw a diagram showing the x- and y-components of the resultant vector to determine the angle and the quadrant in which the vector is located. It is very difficult to determine the location of the vector without the diagram.

3. Relative Velocity (Section 3.3)

Physical phenomena can be observed from different **frames of reference**. The velocity of a ball tossed by a passenger in a moving car will be measured differently by a passenger on the car than by an observer on the sidewalk. In fact, any velocity we measure is **relative**. The velocity of a moving car is measured relative to the ground, and the revolving motion of the Earth around the Sun is relative to the Sun, etc. Relative velocity can be determined with vector addition or subtraction. The symbols used in relative velocity such as v_{cg} (where c stands for car and g stands for ground) means the velocity of *a car relative to the ground.*

Example 3.5: A river has a current with a velocity of 1.5 m/s south. A boat whose speed in still water is 5.0 m/s is directed east across the 100-m-wide river.

(a) How long does it take the boat to reach the opposite shore?

(b) How far downstream will the boat land?

(c) What is the velocity of the boat relative to the shore?

We use the following subscripts:

r = river, b = boat, s = shore.

Solution: Given: $v_{rs} = 1.5$ m/s, $v_{br} = 5.0$ m/s, $y = 100$ m.

Find: (a) t (b) x (c) v_{bs}.

We choose the coordinate system as shown.

(a) From the concept of components of motion, the time it takes the boat to reach the opposite shore is simply $t = \dfrac{y}{v_{br}} = \dfrac{100 \text{ m}}{5.0 \text{ m/s}} = 20$ s.

(b) During the 20 s, the boat travels downstream through a distance of

$x = v_{rs}\,t = (1.5 \text{ m/s})(20 \text{ s}) = 30$ m.

(c) The velocity of the boat *relative to shore* is the vector sum of the velocity of the boat *relative to the river* and the velocity of the river *relative to the shore* (the current). $\mathbf{v}_{bs} = \mathbf{v}_{br} + \mathbf{v}_{rs}$.

Note: The pattern of the subscripts is helpful in problem solving. On the right side of the equation, the two inner subscripts are the same (r). The outer subscripts (b and s) are sequentially the same as those for the relative velocity on the left side of the equation. This pattern is a good check to see if you have written the relative velocity equation correctly!

$$v_{bs} = \sqrt{v_{br}^2 + v_{rs}^2} = \sqrt{(5.0 \text{ m/s})^2 + (1.5 \text{ m/s})^2} = 5.2 \text{ m/s},$$

$$\theta = \tan^{-1}\left(\frac{5.0 \text{ m/s}}{1.5 \text{ m/s}}\right) = 73° \text{ measured from shoreline.}$$

The velocity of the *boat relative to the shore* (or the velocity of the boat measured by an observer standing on the shore) is 5.2 m/s in a direction of 73° measured from the shoreline.

Example 3.6: If the person on the boat in Example 3.5 wants to travel directly across the river,

(a) at what angle upstream must the boat be directed?

(b) with what speed will the boat cross the river?

(c) how long will it take the boat to reach the opposite shore?

Solution:

To travel directly across the river, the velocity of the boat *relative to the shore* must be directly across the river. The vector form of the relative-velocity equation in Example 3.5, $\mathbf{v}_{bs} = \mathbf{v}_{br} + \mathbf{v}_{rs}$ is still valid.

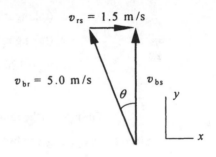

(a) $\theta = \sin^{-1}\dfrac{v_{rs}}{v_{br}} = \sin^{-1}\dfrac{1.5 \text{ m/s}}{5.0 \text{ m/s}} = 17°$ upstream from a line straight

across the river.

(b) From the triangle in the diagram, we have $v_{bs}^2 + v_{rs}^2 = v_{br}^2$,

so $\quad v_{bs} = \sqrt{v_{br}^2 - v_{rs}^2} = \sqrt{(5.0 \text{ m/s})^2 - (1.5 \text{ m/s})^2} = 4.8 \text{ m/s}.$

(c) The time is then $t = \dfrac{y}{v_{bs}} = \dfrac{100 \text{ m}}{4.8 \text{ m/s}} = 21 \text{ s}.$

---

4. Projectile Motion (Section 3.4)

Projectile motion is motion in two dimensions, horizontal and vertical, with the vertical motion under the action of gravity only (downward). Because the action of gravity is in the vertical direction, the horizontal motion has zero acceleration, if air resistance is ignored. The vertical motion is a free fall and so the acceleration is the acceleration due to gravity, $a_y = -g = -9.80 \text{ m/s}^2$, if the upward direction is chosen positive. This two-dimensional motion is analyzed using components; that is, the horizontal quantities are independent of the vertical quantities, and vice versa; however, the time of flight—the time the projectile spends in the air—is the common quantity for both the horizontal and vertical motions.

Applying the general kinematic equations in component form to projectile motion ($a_x = 0$ and $a_y = -g$ with the upward direction chosen positive), we have $v_x = v_{xo}$, $v_y = v_{yo} - gt$, $x = x_o + v_{xo}t$, $y = y_o + v_{yo}t - \frac{1}{2}gt^2$, and so on. Again, the key to success in solving projectile motion is to resolve the motion into components, treat the components as independent, and use the same time of flight for both motions. Always think about resolving vectors into components. Usually, the time of flight is something you have to find first, since it is a common quantity for both motions.

Example 3.7: A package is dropped from an airplane traveling with a constant horizontal speed of 120 m/s at an altitude of 500 m. What is the horizontal distance the package travels before hitting the ground (the range)?

Solution: Given: horizontal motion   vertical motion

      (taking it in the x-direction) (up as positive)

      (taking $x_o = 0$)   (taking $y_o = 0$)

      $v_{xo} = 120$ m/s, $v_{yo} = 0$,

                 $y = -500$ m.

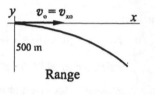

    Find: x (the range).

Since the range is given by $x = x_o + v_{xo}t = v_{xo}t$, we have to find the time of flight t first.

From the vertical motion, we use $y = y_o + v_{yo}t - \frac{1}{2}gt^2 = v_{yo}t - \frac{1}{2}gt^2$.

Thus, -500 m $= 0 - \frac{1}{2}(9.80$ m/s$^2)t^2$, and $t = 10.1$ s.

Therefore, $x = (120$ m/s$)(10.1$ s$) = 1.21 \times 10^3$ m $= 1.21$ km.

Note: The quantities such as initial velocities and displacements have to be treated independently. For example, the initial horizontal velocity is 120 m/s, and the initial vertical velocity is zero. The 120 m/s can be used *only* in the horizontal motion, and the 0 m/s can be used *only* in the vertical motion. A common mistake is to use the 120 m/s for the vertical motion. It is imperative to list the horizontal and vertical quantities separately.

Example 3.8: A golfer hits a golf ball with a velocity of 35 m/s at an angle of 25° above the horizontal. If the point where the ball is hit and the point where the ball lands are at the same level,

    (a) how long is the ball in the air?

    (b) what is the range of the ball?

Solution:

Given: horizontal motion | vertical motion

(taking it in the x-direction) | (up as positive)

(taking $x_o = 0$) | (taking $y_o = 0$)

$v_{xo} = v_o \cos\theta$ | $v_{yo} = v_o \sin\theta$

= (35 m/s) cos 25° | = (35 m/s) sin 25°

= 31.7 m/s; | = 14.8 m/s

$y = 0$ (on landing).

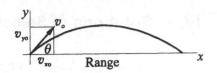

Find: (a) t (b) x.

(a) When the golf ball lands, $y = 0$; and from $y = y_o + v_{yo}t - \frac{1}{2}gt^2$, we have

$$0 = 0 + (14.8 \text{ m/s})t - \frac{1}{2}(9.80 \text{ m/s}^2)t^2.$$

Solving the quadratic equation, we obtain $t = 0$ or 3.02 s.
The $t = 0$ root corresponds to the position at the start ($x_o = 0$ and $y_o = 0$) and the $t = 3.02$ s corresponds to the landing position ($x =$ the range and $y = 0$), so the time of flight is 3.0 s, (to two significant figures).

(b) $x = x_o + v_{xo}t = 0 + (31.7 \text{ m/s})(3.02 \text{ s}) = 96$ m.

III. Mathematical Summary

Components of Initial velocity	$v_x = v\cos\theta$ (3.1a) $v_y = v\sin\theta$ (3.1b)		Relates the x- and y-components to the magnitude and the angle of the initial velocity. (θ is from x-axis)
Components of Displacement	$x = x_o + v_{xo}t + \frac{1}{2}a_x t^2$ (3.3a) $y = y_o + v_{yo}t + \frac{1}{2}a_y t^2$ (3.3b)		Relates the displacement components to initial velocity components, acceleration components, and time (constant acceleration only).
Components of Velocity	$v_x = v_{xo} + a_x t$ (3.3c) $v_y = v_{yo} + a_y t$ (3.3d)		Relates the velocity components to initial velocity components and acceleration components (constant acceleration only).
Vector Representation	$C = \sqrt{C_x^2 + C_y^2}$ (3.4a) $\theta = \tan^{-1}\left|\dfrac{C_y}{C_x}\right|$ (3.6)		Magnitude-angle form.
Vector Representation	$\mathbf{C} = C_x\,\hat{\mathbf{x}} + C_y\,\hat{\mathbf{y}}$ (3.7)		Component form.

IV.   Solutions of Selected Exercises and Paired Exercises

6.   (a) For $\theta < 45°$, $\cos \theta > \sin \theta$. Since $v_x = v \cos \theta$, and $v_y = v \sin \theta$, the horizontal velocity component is $\boxed{\text{greater than}}$ the vertical velocity component.

(b) Horizontal: $v_x = v \cos \theta = (35 \text{ m/s}) \cos 37° = \boxed{28 \text{ m/s}}$.

Vertical: $v_y = v \sin \theta = (35 \text{ m/s}) \sin 37° = \boxed{21 \text{ m/s}}$.

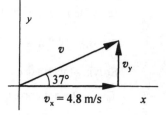

9.   (a) $\cos 37° = \dfrac{v_x}{v} = \dfrac{4.8 \text{ m/s}}{v}$,

so $v = \dfrac{4.8 \text{ m/s}}{\cos 37°} = \boxed{6.0 \text{ m/s}}$.

(b) $v_y = v \sin 37° = (6.0 \text{ m/s}) \sin 37° = \boxed{3.6 \text{ m/s}}$.

10.   (a) From the sketch it is clear that the displacement that will bring the student back to the starting point is pointing from the finishing point to the starting point, so it is $\boxed{\text{north of east}}$.

(b) $d = \sqrt{(50 \text{ m})^2 + (100 \text{ m})^2} = \boxed{1.1 \times 10^2 \text{ m}}$,

$\theta = \tan^{-1}\left(\dfrac{50 \text{ m}}{100 \text{ m}}\right) = \boxed{27° \text{ north of east}}$.

14.   Take both x_o and y_o to be 0. $x = v_x t = (0.60 \text{ m/s})(2.5 \text{ s}) = 1.5 \text{ m}$; $y = v_y t = (0.80 \text{ m/s})(2.5 \text{ s}) = 2.0 \text{ m}$.

$d = \sqrt{x^2 + y^2} = \sqrt{(1.5 \text{ m})^2 + (2.0 \text{ m})^2} = \boxed{2.5 \text{ m}}$.

$\theta = \tan^{-1}\left(\dfrac{2.0 \text{ m}}{1.5 \text{ m}}\right) = \boxed{53° \text{ above } +x\text{-axis}}$.

17. $\sqrt{(3.0 \text{ m})^2 + (4.0 \text{ m})^2} = 5.0 \text{ m}$.

For ball 1, $t = \dfrac{5.0 \text{ m}}{0.75 \text{ m/s}} = 6.67 \text{ s}$.

For ball 2, $v = \dfrac{3.0 \text{ m} + 4.0 \text{ m}}{6.67 \text{ s}} = \boxed{1.0 \text{ m/s}}$.

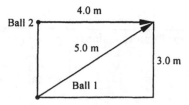

20.   (c). For a triangle, a side can never be smaller than the difference of the other two sides and greater than the sum of the other two sides.

27.   (a) $\boxed{\text{Yes}}$, vector addition is associative.

(b) See the diagrams.

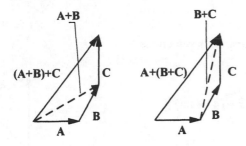

32.   (a) See the diagram.

(b) For the 15-m vector: $d_{1x} = (15\ \text{m}) \cos 45° = 10.6\ \text{m};$

$d_{1y} = (15\ \text{m}) \sin 45° = 10.6\ \text{m}.$

For the 25-m vector: $d_{2x} = 25\ \text{m};$

$d_{2y} = 0.$

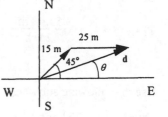

Thus, $d_x = d_{1x} + d_{2x} = 10.6\ \text{m} + 25\ \text{m} = 35.6\ \text{m};$

$d_y = d_{1y} + d_{2y} = 10.6\ \text{m} + 0 = 10.6\ \text{m}.$

Therefore, $d = \sqrt{(35.6\ \text{m})^2 + (10.6\ \text{m})^2} = \boxed{37\ \text{m}},$

$\theta = \tan^{-1}\left(\dfrac{10.6\ \text{m}}{35.6\ \text{m}}\right) = \boxed{17°\ \text{north of east}}.$

37.   (a) $\mathbf{F}_1 = [(12.0\ \text{N}) \cos 37°]\ \hat{\mathbf{x}} + [(12.0\ \text{N}) \sin 37°]\ \hat{\mathbf{y}} = (9.58\ \text{N})\ \hat{\mathbf{x}} + (7.22\ \text{N})\ \hat{\mathbf{y}}.$

$\mathbf{F}_2 = [-(12.0\ \text{N}) \cos 37°]\ \hat{\mathbf{x}} + [(12.0\ \text{N}) \sin 37°]\ \hat{\mathbf{y}} = (-9.58\ \text{N})\ \hat{\mathbf{x}} + (7.22\ \text{N})\ \hat{\mathbf{y}}.$

Thus, $\mathbf{F}_1 + \mathbf{F}_2 = \boxed{(14.4\ \text{N})\ \hat{\mathbf{y}}}.$

(b) $\mathbf{F}_1 = [(12.0\ \text{N}) \cos 27°]\ \hat{\mathbf{x}} + [(12.0\ \text{N}) \sin 27°]\ \hat{\mathbf{y}} = (10.7\ \text{N})\ \hat{\mathbf{x}} + (5.45\ \text{N})\ \hat{\mathbf{y}}.$

Thus, $\mathbf{F}_1 + \mathbf{F}_2 = (1.1\ \text{N})\ \hat{\mathbf{x}} + (12.7\ \text{N})\ \hat{\mathbf{y}}.$

$F_1 + F_2 = \sqrt{(1.1\ \text{N})^2 + (12.7\ \text{N})^2} = \boxed{12.7\ \text{N}}.$ $\theta = \tan^{-1}\left(\dfrac{12.7\ \text{N}}{1.1\ \text{N}}\right) = \boxed{85.0°\ \text{above} +x\text{-axis}}.$

42.   From $\mathbf{F}_1 + \mathbf{F}_2 + \mathbf{F}_3 = 0,$

$\mathbf{F}_3 = -\mathbf{F}_1 - \mathbf{F}_2 = (-3.0\ \text{N})\ \hat{\mathbf{x}} + (-3.0\ \text{N})\ \hat{\mathbf{y}} - [(-6.0\ \text{N})\ \hat{\mathbf{x}} + (4.5\ \text{N})\ \hat{\mathbf{y}}] = (3.0\ \text{N})\ \hat{\mathbf{x}} + (-1.5\ \text{N})\ \hat{\mathbf{y}}.$

Therefore, $F_3 = \sqrt{(3.0\ \text{N})^2 + (-1.5\ \text{N})^2} = \boxed{3.4\ \text{N}}$, and $\theta = \tan^{-1}\left(\dfrac{-1.5\ \text{N}}{3.0\ \text{N}}\right) = \boxed{27°\ \text{below the} +x\text{-axis}}.$

45. In the triangle, $F_\parallel$ is opposite and $F_\perp$ is adjacent to the 37° angle.

So $\quad F_\parallel = (50\ \text{N}) \sin 37° = \boxed{30\ \text{N}}$,

$\qquad F_\perp = (50\ \text{N}) \cos 37° = \boxed{40\ \text{N}}$.

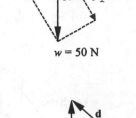

48. (a) From the sketch, the general direction of the thunderstorm's velocity is $\boxed{\text{north of west}}$.

(b) $\mathbf{d}_1 = (60\ \text{mi})[(\cos 45°)\ \hat{\mathbf{x}} + (\sin 45°)\ \hat{\mathbf{y}}] = (42.4\ \text{mi})\ \hat{\mathbf{x}} + (42.4\ \text{mi})\ \hat{\mathbf{y}}$.

$\mathbf{d}_2 = (75\ \text{mi})\ \hat{\mathbf{y}}$.

$\mathbf{d} = \mathbf{d}_2 - \mathbf{d}_1 = (75\ \text{mi})\ \hat{\mathbf{y}} - [(42.4\ \text{mi})\ \hat{\mathbf{x}} + (42.4\ \text{mi})\ \hat{\mathbf{y}}] = (-42.4\ \text{mi})\ \hat{\mathbf{x}} + (32.6\ \text{mi})\ \hat{\mathbf{y}}$.

So $\quad d = \sqrt{(-42.4\ \text{mi})^2 + (32.6\ \text{mi})^2} = 53.48\ \text{mi}$.

Therefore $\quad v = \dfrac{53.48\ \text{mi}}{2.0\ \text{h}} = \boxed{26.7\ \text{mi/h}}$. $\qquad \theta = \tan^{-1}\left(\dfrac{32.6\ \text{mi}}{-42.4\ \text{mi}}\right) = \boxed{37.6°\ \text{north of west}}$.

58. Use the following subscripts: t = truck, b = ball, and o = observer.

Thus, $\quad v_{tg} = 70\ \text{km/h}$, $\quad v_{bt} = -15\ \text{km/h}$.

(a) $v_{bo} = v_{bt} + v_{to} = -15\ \text{km/h} + 70\ \text{km/h} = \boxed{+55\ \text{km/h}}$.

(b) $v_{bt} = v_{bo} - v_{to} = 55\ \text{km/h} - 90\ \text{km/h} = \boxed{-35\ \text{km/h}}$.

61. Use the following subscripts: b = boat, c = current, and w = water.

Upstream: $\quad v_{bc} = 7.5\ \text{m/s}$, $\quad v_{cw} = -5.0\ \text{m/s}$.

$v_{bw} = v_{bc} + v_{cw} = 7.5\ \text{m/s} + (-5.0\ \text{m/s}) = 2.5\ \text{m/s}$, $\quad$ so $\quad t_{up} = \dfrac{500\ \text{m}}{2.5\ \text{m/s}} = 200\ \text{s}$.

Downstream: $\quad v_{bc} = 7.5\ \text{m/s}$, $\quad v_{cw} = 5.0\ \text{m/s}$. $\quad v_{bw} = v_{bc} + v_{cw} = 7.5\ \text{m/s} + 5.0\ \text{m/s} = 12.5\ \text{m/s}$,

so $\quad t_{down} = \dfrac{500\ \text{m}}{12.5\ \text{m/s}} = 40\ \text{s}$. $\quad$ Therefore, $t = 200\ \text{s} + 40\ \text{s} = 240\ \text{s} = \boxed{4.0\ \text{min}}$.

64. (a) From the sketch, the general direction of the swimmer's velocity, relative to the river bank, is $\boxed{\text{north of east}}$.

Use the following subscripts: s = swimmer, c = current, and b = bank.

$\mathbf{v}_{sb} = \mathbf{v}_{sc} + \mathbf{v}_{cb}$.

Thus, $\quad v_{sb} = \sqrt{(0.20\ \text{m/s})^2 + (0.15\ \text{m/s})^2} = \boxed{0.25\ \text{m/s}}$.

$\theta = \tan^{-1}\left(\dfrac{0.15\ \text{m/s}}{0.20\ \text{m/s}}\right) = \boxed{37°\ \text{north of east}}$.

72. The horizontal motion does not affect the vertical motion. The vertical motion of the ball projected horizontally is identical with that of the ball dropped.

76. Given: $v_{xo} = 15$ m/s, $v_{yo} = 0$, $y = -6.0$ m. Find: x. (taking both x_o and y_o as 0)

First find the time of flight from the vertical motion.

From $y = y_o + v_{yo}t - \frac{1}{2}gt^2 = 0 - \frac{1}{2}gt^2$, we have $t = \sqrt{-\frac{2y}{g}} = \sqrt{-\frac{2(-6.0 \text{ m})}{9.80 \text{ m/s}^2}} = 1.11$ s.

$x = x_o + v_{xo}t = 0 + (15 \text{ m/s})(1.11 \text{ s}) = \boxed{17 \text{ m}}$.

81. (a) $\boxed{\text{Ball B collides with ball A}}$ because they have the same horizontal velocity.

(b) (taking both x_o and y_o as 0)

From $y = y_o + v_{yo}t - \frac{1}{2}gt^2 = 0 - \frac{1}{2}gt^2$, we have $t = \sqrt{-\frac{2y}{g}} = \sqrt{-\frac{2(-1.00 \text{ m})}{9.80 \text{ m/s}^2}} = 0.452$ s.

$x = x_o + v_{xo}t = 0 + (0.25 \text{ m/s})(0.452 \text{ s}) = \boxed{0.11 \text{ m}}$ for both.

84. $v_{xo} = v_o \cos\theta = (20.0 \text{ m/s}) \cos 15.0° = 19.32$ m/s, $v_{yo} = v_o \sin\theta = (20.0 \text{ m/s}) \sin 15.0° = 5.176$ m/s.

(taking both x_o and y_o as 0)

(a) At maximum height, $v_y = 0$. From $v_y^2 = v_{yo}^2 - 2g(y - y_o)$, we have $y = \frac{(5.176 \text{ m/s})^2}{2(9.80 \text{ m/s}^2)} = \boxed{1.37 \text{ m}}$.

(b) At impact, $y = 0$. From $y = y_o + v_{yo}t - \frac{1}{2}gt^2$, we have $t = \frac{5.176 \text{ m/s}}{\frac{1}{2}(9.80 \text{ m/s}^2)} = 1.056$ s.

Thus, $R = x = x_o + v_{xo}t = 0 + (19.32 \text{ m/s})(1.056 \text{ s}) = \boxed{20.4 \text{ m}}$.

(c) Kick the ball harder to $\boxed{\text{increase } v_o \text{ and/or increase the angle}}$, so as close to 45° as possible.

87. (taking both x_o and y_o as 0)

From $y = y_o + v_{yo}t - \frac{1}{2}gt^2$, we have $0 = 0 + v_{yo}t - \frac{1}{2}gt^2$, so $t = \frac{2v_{yo}}{g} = \frac{2v_o \sin\theta}{g}$.

$R = x = x_o + v_{xo}t = 0 + v_o \cos\theta \, t = v_o \cos\theta \frac{2v_o \sin\theta}{g} = \frac{2v_o^2 \sin\theta \cos\theta}{g} = \frac{v_o^2 \sin 2\theta}{g}$.

Therefore, $\sin 2\theta = \frac{Rg}{v_o^2} = \frac{(31 \text{ m})(9.80 \text{ m/s}^2)}{(18 \text{ m/s})^2} = 0.937$.

Thus, $2\theta = \sin^{-1}(0.938) = 69.7°$ or $110°$. Hence, $\theta = \boxed{35° \text{ or } 55°}$.

90.   Use the result from Exercise 3.87.

The range $R = 15$ m,   so $R = \dfrac{v_o^2 \sin 2\theta}{g} = 15$ m.

That is, $R = \dfrac{(55 \text{ m/s})^2 \sin 2\theta}{9.80 \text{ m/s}^2} = 15$ m,   or $\sin 2\theta = 0.0486$.

Therefore, $2\theta = \sin^{-1}(0.0486) = 2.79°$;   hence, $\theta = \boxed{1.4°}$.

V.   Practice Quiz

1.   The resultant of two vectors is greatest when the angle between them is
   (a) 0°   (b) 45°   (c) 60°   (d) 90°   (e) 180°

2.   If a ball is thrown with a velocity of 25 m/s at an angle of 37° above the horizontal, what is the vertical component of the velocity?
   (a) 25 m/s   (b) 20 m/s   (c) 18 m/s   (d) 15 m/s   (e) 10 m/s

3.   An object is moving in the x-y plane. The acceleration in the x- and y-directions is 1.0 m/s^2 and 3.0 m/s^2, respectively. If the object starts from rest, what are its coordinates at $t = 4.0$ s?
   (a) (8.0 m, 24 m)   (b) (24 m, 8.0 m)   (c) (4.0 m, 12 m)   (d) (12 m, 4.0 m)   (e) (8.0 m, 12 m)

4.   A boat whose speed in still water is 8.0 m/s is directed across a river with a current of 6.0 m/s along the shore. What is the speed of the boat relative to the shore as it crosses the river?
   (a) 2.7 m/s   (b) 5.3 m/s   (c) 6.0 m/s   (d) 8.0 m/s   (e) 10 m/s

5.   Find the resultant of the following vectors:
   $v_1 = (2.0 \text{ m/s}) \, \hat{x} + (3.0 \text{ m/s}) \, \hat{y}$, $v_2 = (-4.0 \text{ m/s}) \, \hat{x} + (7.0 \text{ m/s}) \, \hat{y}$, $v_3 = 10$ m/s, 37° above the −x-axis.
   (a) 19 m/s, 58° above the +x-axis   (b) 19 m/s, 58° above the −x-axis
   (c) 19 m/s, 22° above the +x axis   (d) 19 m/s, 22° above the −x axis
   (e) none of the preceding

6.   A stone is thrown horizontally with an initial speed of 8.0 m/s from the edge of a cliff. A stopwatch measures the stone's trajectory time from the top of the cliff to the bottom to be 3.4 s. What is the height of the cliff?
   (a) 17 m   (b) 27 m   (c) 34 m   (d) 57 m   (e) 1.1×10^2 m

7. An Olympic long-jumper goes into the jump with a speed of 10 m/s at an angle of 30° above the horizontal. How far is the jump?

   (a) 1.0 m   (b) 5.0 m   (c) 8.7 m   (d) 9.8 m   (e) 10 m

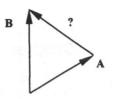

8. The resultant shown in the vector diagram is for

   (a) **A** + **B**.   (b) **A** − **B**.   (c) **B** + **A**.   (d) **B** − **A**.   (e) **A** × **B**.

9. You are traveling at +55 mi/h relative to a straight, level road and pass a car traveling at +45 mi/h. The velocity of your car relative to the other car is

   (a) 10 mi/h.   (b) −10 mi/h.   (c) 65 mi/h.   (d) 35 mi/h.   (e) 100 mi/h.

10. The football field for your college team is 10 km at 30° north of east from your residence. You first drive 3.0 km north to go to a store. What should be your next displacement so you can go to the football game?

    (a) 13 km at 8.9° north of east   (b) 8.9 km at 13° north of east   (c) 7.0 km at 30° north of east

    (d) 7.0 km at 60° north of east   (e) 12 km at 43°° north of east

11. A small boat can maintain a speed of 1.5 m/s in still water. In order to directly cross a river in which there is a 0.75 m/s current, at what upstream angle must the boat head?

    (a) 15°.   (b) 27°.   (c) 30°.   (d) 60°.   (e) 63°.

12. A golf ball is hit at a speed of 30 m/s at an angle of 30° above the horizontal. What is the maximum height reached by the golf ball?

    (a) 0.51 m.   (b) 1.5 m.   (c) 11 m.   (d) 34 m.   (e) 46 m.

Answers to Practice Quiz:

1.a 2.d 3.a 4.e 5.b 6.d 7.c 8.d 9.a 10.b 11.c 12.c

CHAPTER 4

Force and Motion

I. Chapter Objectives

Upon completion of this chapter, you should be able to:

1. relate force and motion and explain what is meant by a net or unbalanced force.

2. state and explain Newton's first law of motion and describe inertia and its relationship to mass.

3. state and explain Newton's second law of motion, apply it to physical situations, and distinguish between weight and mass.

4. state and explain Newton's third law of motion and identify action–reaction force pairs.

5. apply Newton's second law in analyzing various situations, use free-body diagrams, and understand the concept of translational equilibrium.

6. explain the causes of friction and how friction is described by using coefficients of friction.

II. Chapter Summary and Discussion

1. Force and Net Force (Section 4.1)

Force (**F**) is the cause of *acceleration* or change in velocity, and it is the technical term for what we commonly call a push, pull, kick, or shove. Force is a vector quantity (it has both magnitude and direction). There must be a **net force** (unbalanced force) acting on an object for the object to change its velocity (either magnitude and/or direction) or to accelerate.

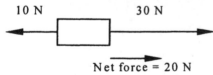

Net Force. ΣF or $\mathbf{F}_{net}$, is the vector sum, the resultant, or the unbalanced force acting on an object. Here the symbol Σ means "the sum of." ΣF means the vector sum of forces. The unit of force in SI is a combination of the fundamental units of mass, length, and time and is called **newton** (N). 1 N is the net force required to accelerate a mass of 1 kg with an acceleration of 1 m/s² or, $1 \text{ N} = 1 \text{ kg} \cdot \text{m/s}^2$. For example, as illustrated in the preceding diagram, two forces, 10 N and 30 N, are acting on an object in opposite directions. There are two forces on the object; however, there is only one net force (the resultant of the vector sum of the two forces) of 20 N (to the right) acting on the object.

Note: The net force is *not* a separate force. It is simply the vector sum of the individual forces.

To analyze the forces acting on an object, you should draw a **free-body diagram** (there is more on free-body diagram later in Section 4.5 in the textbook). A free-body diagram can be drawn by

(1)   isolating the object of interest (this should be the only object in the diagram).

(2)   drawing all the forces acting on the object as vectors (including directions).

Example 4.1:   Draw a free-body diagram of a book sitting on a horizontal desk.

Solution:

First we isolate the book and analyze the forces acting on the book. There are two forces acting on the book, the gravitational force (or weight) and the supporting force on the book by the horizontal desk. First, the gravitational force (an action-at-a-distance force with no physical contact) is always present if we are dealing with objects on the Earth. Second, whenever an object makes a physical contact with another object, a force results. Here the book makes a contact with the desk, so there is a supporting force. In most cases, these contact forces are perpendicular to the contact surface and therefore are called **normal forces** (N).

As a follow-up to this example, try to draw a free-body diagram of an object sliding freely on a frictionless inclined ramp.

---

2.   Newton's Laws of Motion (Sections 4.2 – 4.4)

(1)   **Newton's first law** describes the state of motion of an object when there is *no net force* (net force equals zero) acting on the object.

An object at rest will remain at rest and an object in motion will keep moving with constant velocity if the net force on the object is zero.

An object at rest has no change in velocity (its velocity is zero all the time), so its acceleration is zero. An object moving with constant velocity (same speed and same direction) has no change in velocity either, and its acceleration is also zero. Therefore, Newton's first law can be summarized in a very simple relation:

If $\Sigma F = 0$, then v = constant (zero is just a special case of constant velocity), or $a = 0$.

Note: Newton's first law is often called the *law of inertia*. **Inertia** is the natural tendency of an object to resist acceleration or change in motion, and it is measured quantitatively by its mass.

A common misconception about Newton's first law is that a force is required to keep an object in motion. This is not so. Experiments done on air tracks (where there is negligible friction) show that no force is required to keep an object moving with constant velocity. We get this misconception because friction is always present in our everyday lives. To maintain constant velocity of a moving car, you have to push on the accelerator. Does this contradict Newton's first law? No! It is seen clearly in the preceding diagram that the forward force on the car is equal in magnitude and opposite to the backward friction force (air friction plus ground friction), and so they cancel each other, resulting in a zero net force. Therefore, there is no net force on the car, and the car moves away with constant velocity.

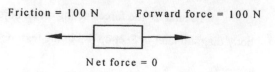

What happens if the *net force is not zero*? Newton's second law describes the relation among force, mass, and acceleration when there is a non-zero net force on an object.

(2)   **Newton's second law** states that the acceleration depends on the net force ΣF and on the mass m of the object (note that it is *net force* here, not just force). Mathematically, this law is equivalent to

$$a = \frac{\Sigma F}{m} \quad \text{or} \quad \Sigma F = ma.$$

If you think of inertia as the qualitative term for the tendency of a body that resists acceleration, then **mass** (a scalar quantity) is the quantitative measure of inertia. If the mass is large, the acceleration produced by a given net force will be small.

Newton's second law is a vector equation. Note that acceleration **a** is in the direction of the net force ΣF, not necessarily in the direction of velocity **v**. You must include *all* the forces acting on an object to determine the net force and then the acceleration. However, often you will find that a force on an object is balanced by an equal and opposite force, such as weight balanced by a normal force of a book on a desk. Because this pair of forces cancels, you do not necessarily have to include them in your calculation.

Example 4.2:   A 5.0-N horizontal force pulls a 20-kg box on a horizontal surface. A 3.0-N friction force retards the motion. What is the acceleration of the object?

Solution: Given: $m = 20$ kg, F (pulling) = 5.0 N, f (friction) = 3.0 N.
          Find: **a**.

First we draw a free-body diagram of the box. The two vertical forces, $w = mg$ and N, are equal and opposite (if they were not, the box would accelerate up or down). $\Sigma F_y = N - w = ma_y = 0$ and we do not need to include them in our calculation. Thus, we have only

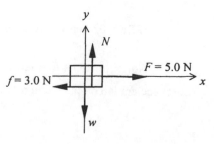

two forces, 5.0 N to the right and 3.0 N to the left, to deal with. The net force in this case is (taking the direction of **F** as positive):

$\Sigma F = F - f = 5.0\ N - 3.0\ N = 2.0\ N$ (to the right or $+x$).

Hence, the acceleration of the object is $\mathbf{a} = \dfrac{\Sigma F}{m} = \dfrac{2.0\ N}{20\ kg} = 0.10\ m/s^2$ (to the right, or $+x$).

If you apply Newton's second law to gravity near the Earth's surface, you get the relation among weight w (gravitational force), mass m, and gravitational acceleration g: $w = mg$.

Example 4.3:   Find the weight of a 3.50-kg object.

Solution: Given: $m = 3.50$ kg.   Find: w.

We use the relation $w = mg = (3.50\ kg)(9.80\ m/s^2\ downward) = 34.3\ N\ downward$.

Note: Weight and mass are two very different physical quantities. Mass is a measure of the inertia or resistance to change in motion of an object. Mass is a constant for a given object, so it is independent of where the mass is located. For example, a 5.0-kg mass on the Earth still has a mass of 5.0 kg on the Moon. Weight is the gravitational force acting on an object and depends on the acceleration due to gravity at a location and mass. For example, a 5.0-kg mass has a weight of $(5.0\ kg)(9.80\ m/s^2) = 49\ N$ on the Earth, $(5.0\ kg)(1.67\ m/s^2) = 8.4\ N$ on the Moon, and *zero* in deep space far away from any object (why?).

(3)   **Newton's third law** states that if object 1 exerts a force on object 2, then object 2 exerts an equal and opposite force on object 1. In mathematical terms, the law can be written as $\mathbf{F}_{12} = -\mathbf{F}_{21}$. (See the following sketch for Newton's third law.)

The negative sign in the preceding relation simply means that $\mathbf{F}_{12}$ is opposite $\mathbf{F}_{21}$. The notation $\mathbf{F}_{12}$ stands for the force on object 1 by object 2.

The force by object 1 is *on* object 2, and the force by object 2 is *on* object 1, so the two forces are always acting on *two different* objects. Therefore, even though these two forces are equal and opposite, they *do not* cancel each other because of this fact. If you analyze only object 1 or object 2 in the diagram, there is only *one* force acting, and both objects will accelerate, in opposite directions, though.

Newton's third law is often called the *law of action and reaction*. The first force, for example, the force by object 1, is called the action force, and the second force, the force by object 2, is then called the reaction force.

There is another misconception concerning the third law. The third law states that the two forces are *equal* no matter what. For example, if an egg and a stone collide with each other, the egg breaks and the stone remains intact. Because the egg breaks, we often conclude that the force by the stone on the egg is greater than the force by the egg on the stone. This is not so. The forces are always equal. The egg breaks because it is simply easier to break. It takes a smaller force to break the egg than to break the stone.

Example 4.4:   A large truck collides head-on with a small car and causes a lot of damage to the small car. Because there is more damage to the small car than to the large truck,

(a) the force on the truck is greater in magnitude than the force on the car,

(b) the force on the truck is equal in magnitude to the force on the car, ⟵

(c) the force on the truck is smaller in magnitude than the force on the car,

(d) the force on the truck is in the same direction as the force on the car.

(e) the truck did not slow down during the collision.

Solution:

According to Newton's third law, the answer is (b). Why isn't answer (c) correct, since the truck causes more damage on the car? It takes a smaller force to damage a small car than to damage a large truck. When the truck and the car collide, they exert forces that are equal in magnitude but opposite in direction on each other, say 15 000 N. It may take only 10 000 N to damage the bumper on the car and 20 000 N to damage the bumper on the truck. Thus, the car gets damaged and the truck remains basically undamaged, even though the force by the car on the truck is of the same magnitude as the force on the car by the truck.

Answer (e) is also wrong, as the truck *did* slow down from the force by the car because it is opposite the truck's velocity.

---

3.   Application of Newton's Laws (Section 4.5)

When it comes to applying Newton's three laws of motion to various mechanical systems, there is no short cut to take. You *must* follow a certain set of procedures to analyze and solve the unknown physical quantities. Here is a simplified version of the procedures outlined in the textbook:

(1)   Draw a free-body diagram for each object involved in the analysis.

(2)   Select a rectangular coordinate system. The solutions will be much easier if you select the $+x$-axis in the direction of acceleration and the $+y$-axis perpendicular to the x-axis.

(3)   Resolve all forces not pointing in the x- or y-direction into their x- and y-components, respectively.

(4)   Add, algebraically, all the x-components and y-components of the forces, respectively.

(5)   Set $\Sigma F_x = ma$ and $\Sigma F_y = 0$ and solve for the unknown quantities.

Because you have chosen the $+x$-axis in the direction of acceleration, the object will not accelerate in the y-direction. That is why the acceleration in the y-direction is zero, and $\Sigma F_y = ma_y = 0$.

Do these steps sound familiar? In essence, these are the same procedures we followed when we added vectors using the analytical component method. Our goal here is to find the net force and then the acceleration. Because force is a vector, the method really boils down to adding vectors.

Example 4.5:   A student pulls a box of books on a smooth horizontal floor with a 100-N force in a direction of 37° above the horizontal surface. If the mass of the box (with the books) is 40.0 kg, what is the acceleration of the box and the normal force on the box by the floor?

Solution: Given: $F = 100$ N, $\theta = 37°$, $m = 40.0$ kg.

Find: a and N.

(1) Free-body diagram:

Because the box is on the Earth, it has a weight of $w = mg$ pointing toward the center of the earth (or perpendicular to the horizontal direction). The box is also making physical contacts with the floor and the student, so there are two contact forces. The contact force with the floor is a normal force (N) and is directed straight upward perpendicular to the contact surface. The force by the student, F, is directed at 37° above the horizontal direction (smooth floor implies negligible friction).

(2) Coordinate system:

Even though the student is pulling at an angle above the horizontal direction, the box will still move or accelerate along the horizontal direction. Tgus, we choose the horizontal direction (to the right) as the $+x$-axis and the vertical direction (upward) as the $+y$-axis.

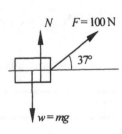

(3) x- and y-components:

Among the three forces, only the student's pulling force is not completely along either the x- or the y-axis, so we need to find its x- and y-components. From trigonometry, we can see that the x-component is adjacent to the 37° angle, and the y-component is opposite the 37° angle. Therefore, we use cos 37° to calculate the x-component and sin 37° to calculate the y-component.

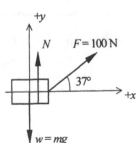

$$F_x = F \cos 37° = (100 \text{ N}) \cos 37° = 80.0 \text{ N};$$

$$F_y = F \sin 37° = (100 \text{ N}) \sin 37° = 60.0 \text{ N}.$$

(4) Adding x- and y-components, respectively:

In the x-direction, there is only one force, the x-component of the student's pulling force, 80 N. In the y-direction, there are three forces: the upward normal force N, the upward y-component of the student's pulling force (60 N), and the downward weight of the box of

$$w = mg = (40.0 \text{ kg})(9.80 \text{ m/s}^2) = 392 \text{ N}.$$

Thus, $\quad \Sigma F_x = 80.0 \text{ N}$ and $\Sigma F_y = N + 60.0 \text{ N} - w = N + 60.0 \text{ N} - 392 \text{ N} = N - 332 \text{ N}.$

(5) Setting $\Sigma F_x = ma$ and $\Sigma F_y = 0$ and solving for the unknown quantities:

$$\Sigma F_x = 80.0 \text{ N} = ma = (40.0 \text{ kg})a, \qquad (1)$$

and

$$\Sigma F_y = N - 332 \text{ N} = 0. \qquad (2)$$

From Eq. (1), we have $a = \dfrac{80.0 \text{ N}}{40.0 \text{ kg}} = 2.00 \text{ m/s}^2.$

From Eq. (2), we have $N = 332$ N.

Note in this case, that the normal force (332 N) is not equal to the weight of the box (392 N). Why?

Example 4.6: A 5.0-kg box, starting from rest, slides down a smooth 37° inclined plane.

(a) Find the acceleration of the box and the normal force by the inclined plane on the box.

(b) If the inclined plane is 10 m long, what will be speed of the box at the bottom of the plane?

Solution: Given: $m = 5,0$ kg, $\theta = 37°$, $v_0 = 0$, $x = 10$ m.

Find: (a) a and N.

(b) v.

(a)

(1) Free-body diagram:

Because the box is on the Earth, it has a weight of $w = mg$ pointing toward the center of the Earth (or perpendicular to the horizontal direction). The box is also making a physical contact with the inclined plane, so there is a contact force (normal force) perpendicular to the inclined plane.

(2) Coordinate system:

Because the box slides down the inclined plane, we choose the $+x$-axis down the inclined plane and the $+y$-axis perpendicular to the inclined plane.

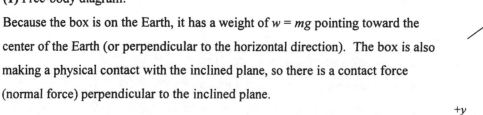

(3) x- and y-components:

The weight of the box, $w = mg$, is not along either the x-axis or the y-axis, so we need to find its x- and y-components. From trigonometry, we can see that the x-component is opposite to the 37° angle, and the y-component is adjacent to the 37° angle.

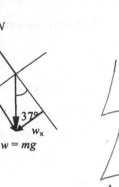

$W_x = w \sin 37° = mg \sin 37°$ and $w_y = w \cos 37° = mg \cos 37°$.

(4) Adding x- and y-components, respectively:

In the x-direction, there is only one force, w_x. $\Sigma F_x = mg \sin 37° = mg \sin 37°$.

In the y-direction, there are two forces, N and w_y. $\Sigma F_x = N - mg \cos 37°$.

(5) Setting $\Sigma F_x = ma$ and $\Sigma F_y = 0$ and solving for the unknown quantities:

$$\Sigma F_x = mg \sin 37° = ma, \qquad\qquad (1)$$

and $\qquad\qquad \Sigma F_y = N - mg \cos 37°. \qquad\qquad (2)$

From Eq. (1), we have $a = g \sin 37° = (9.80 \text{ m/s}^2) \sin 37° = 5.9 \text{ m/s}^2$.

From Eq. (2), we have $N = mg \cos 37° = (5.0 \text{ kg})(9.80 \text{ m/s}^2) \cos 37° = 39 \text{ N}$.

(b) Because velocity is a kinematic quantity, we need to use one of the kinematic equations. (Take $x_0 = 0$.)

From $v^2 = v_0^2 + 2a(x - x_0) = (0)^2 + 2(5.9 \text{ m/s}^2)(10 \text{ m}) = 118 \text{ m}^2/\text{s}^2$,   so $v = 11 \text{ m/s}$.

If there are *no forces* acting on an object, or if there are *equal and opposite forces* acting on an object, the net force on the object *is zero* and the object *will not* accelerate. This state of motion is called **translational equilibrium**. If the system is in equilibrium, we can set $\Sigma \mathbf{F} = 0$, that is, $\Sigma F_x = 0$ and $\Sigma F_y = 0$ in component forms, and then solve for unknown quantities.

Translational equilibrium is a special application of Newton's laws ($\mathbf{a} = 0$). The problem-solving procedure is the same as described in Examples 4.5 and 4.6. The only minor difference is in step **(5)**. Instead of setting $\Sigma F_x = ma$ and $\Sigma F_y = 0$, we set both $\Sigma F_x = 0$ and $\Sigma F_y = 0$, and solve for the unknown quantities.

4.   Friction (Section 4.6)

Consider one object in contact with another, such as a book on a desk. Suppose that the desk is stationary and that the book is either *sliding* or *on the verge of sliding* on the desk. There is interaction between the book and the desk based on intermolecular attractions and repulsions. It is convenient, however, to consider the interaction as if it were two independent ones: one perpendicular to the contact surface (the *normal* force mentioned earlier) and another one parallel to the contact surface, which is called *force of friction* or *friction force*.

There are two kinds of friction forces: static friction and kinetic friction. Static friction force ($f_s \leq \mu_s N$) is parallel to the contact surface when there is *no relative motion* between the objects in contact and kinetic friction force ($f_k = \mu_k N$) is also parallel to the contact surface when there is *relative motion* between objects in contact. Here μ_s is called the coefficient of static friction and μ_k the coefficient of kinetic friction. They are basically measures of the strengths of the molecular interactions or the "roughness" of the contact surface. N is the normal force.

Kinetic friction force doesn't cause much conceptual difficulty, but static friction force is often misunderstood and therefore incorrectly interpreted. If a book is at rest on a desk and no forces with horizontal components are applied to the book, there is *no* static friction force. Suppose, however, that a small horizontal force is applied to the book, but the book remains at rest. We must conclude then that an equal and opposite force acts on the book to prevent it from moving. This is the static friction force. If the horizontally applied force increases, the static friction force will increase by the same amount until its maximum value is reached ($f_{s_{max}} = \mu_s N$). Thus, the static friction force is *not* a fixed value but is dependent on the applied force, with an upper limit of $f_{s_{max}} = \mu_s N$.

Another misconception about static friction force is about its direction. Somehow we have the idea that friction force is always opposite the direction of motion. This is always true only if the friction force is kinetic. Static friction force can be in directions other than opposite the motion. Think about a machine part moving on a conveyor belt in a factory and a car turning on a flat surface. What is moving the part and turning the car? It is static friction force. The static friction force is in the direction of motion on the machine part and perpendicular to the direction of motion on the car. Think carefully when you walk the next time. What enables you to walk? In which direction is that force? (*Hint*: Why is it difficult to walk on ice? Is it possible to walk on a perfectly smooth surface?)

Example 4.7:   The coefficients of static and kinetic friction between a 3.0-kg box and a desk are 0.40, and 0.30, respectively. What is the net force on the box when each of the following horizontal forces is applied to the box? (a) 5.0 N,   (b) 10 N,   (c) 15 N.

Solution: Given: $\mu_s = 0.40$, $\mu_k = 0.30$, $m = 3.0$ kg. $F = 5.0$ N (a),   10 N (b),   15 N (c).
Find: ΣF (net force) in (a), (b), and (c).

From the discussion about friction forces, we know that if the applied force is greater than the maximum static friction force, the box will accelerate. Because both static and kinetic forces depend on the normal force, we must find it first. Applying Newton's second law in the vertical direction, we obtain

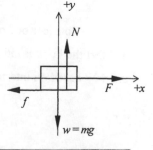

$\Sigma F_y = N - w = ma_y = 0$,

so the normal force between the box and the desk is

$N = w = mg = (3.0 \text{ kg})(9.80 \text{ m/s}^2) = 29.4 \text{ N}$.

The maximum static friction force is then $f_{s_{max}} = \mu_s N = 0.40(29.4 \text{ N}) = 11.8 \text{ N}$.

(a) Because the applied force of 5.0 N is smaller than 11.8 N, the maximum static friction force, the object remains at rest, and therefore the net force is zero.

(b) The applied force is still smaller than the maximum static friction force, and the net force is still zero.

(c) Now the applied force of 15 N is greater than the maximum static friction force, so the object will accelerate, and there is a relative motion along the contact surface. Therefore, we need to replace the static friction force with the kinetic friction force:

$$f_k = \mu_k N = 0.30(29.4 \text{ N}) = 8.82 \text{ N}.$$

Hence, the net force is $\Sigma F = 15 \text{ N} - 8.82 \text{ N} = 6.18 \text{ N}$, and the box will accelerate at a rate of

$$a = \frac{\Sigma F}{m} = \frac{6.18 \text{ N}}{3.0 \text{ kg}} = 2.1 \text{ m/s}^2.$$

The direction of the acceleration is in the same direction as the horizontal force.

III.   Mathematical Summary

Newton's second law	$\Sigma \mathbf{F}_i = \mathbf{F}_{net} = m\mathbf{a}$ (4.1) (*Note*: It is a vector equation)	Relates acceleration with mass and net force when the net force is not zero.
Weight and mass	$w = mg$ (4.2)	Relates weight (gravitational force) with mass and gravitational acceleration.
Component form of Newton's second law	$\Sigma F_x = ma_x$ (4.3b) $\Sigma F_y = ma_y$ (4.3b)	Relates acceleration with mass and force in a particular direction.
Translational Equilibrium condition	$\Sigma \mathbf{F}_i = 0$ (4.4) $\Sigma F_x = 0$ and $\Sigma F_y = 0$ (4.5)	The conditions an object must satisfy if it has zero acceleration.
Force of static friction	$f_s \le \mu_s N$ (4.6) $f_{s_{max}} = \mu_s N$ (4.7) (*Note*: f_s is not a fixed value)	Calculates the static friction force when there is no relative motion along the contact surface.
Force of kinetic friction	$f_k = \mu_k N$ (4.8) (*Note*: f_k is a fixed value)	Calculates the kinetic friction force when there is a relative motion along the contact surface.

IV. Solutions of Selected Exercises and Paired Exercises

8.   The bubble moves ⟨forward⟩ in the direction of velocity or acceleration, because the inertia of the liquid will resist the forward acceleration. Thus, the bubble of negligible mass or inertia moves forward relative to the liquid, then it moves ⟨backward⟩ opposite the velocity (or in the direction of acceleration) for the same reason.

(b) The principle is based on the ⟨inertia of the liquid⟩.

11.   According to Newton's first law or the law of inertia, the dishes at rest tend to remain at rest. For the dishes to move, a static force (discussed in Section 4.6) is required. The quick pull of the tablecloth requires a force that exceeds the maximum static friction so the cloth can move relative to the dishes.

14.   (a) ⟨Either (1) or (2) is possible⟩ because "at rest" or "constant velocity" both have zero acceleration.

(b) $\mathbf{F}_1 = (3.6 \text{ N})[(\cos 74°)\,\hat{\mathbf{x}} - (\sin 74°)\,\hat{\mathbf{y}}] = (0.99 \text{ N})\,\hat{\mathbf{x}} + (-3.46 \text{ N})\,\hat{\mathbf{y}}$.

$\mathbf{F}_2 = (3.6 \text{ N})[(-\cos 34°)\,\hat{\mathbf{x}} + (\sin 34°)\,\hat{\mathbf{y}}] = (-2.98 \text{ N})\,\hat{\mathbf{x}} + (2.01 \text{ N})\,\hat{\mathbf{y}}$.

If $a = 0$, then $\Sigma \mathbf{F} = 0$ from Newton's first law. $\Sigma \mathbf{F} = \mathbf{F}_1 + \mathbf{F}_2 = (-1.99 \text{ N})\,\hat{\mathbf{x}} + (-1.45 \text{ N})\,\mathbf{y} \neq 0$,

so the answer is ⟨yes⟩, there must be a third force to make $\Sigma \mathbf{F} = 0$.

Since $\Sigma \mathbf{F} = \mathbf{F}_1 + \mathbf{F}_2 + \mathbf{F}_3 = 0$, $\mathbf{F}_3 = -(\mathbf{F}_1 + \mathbf{F}_2) = (1.99 \text{ N})\,\hat{\mathbf{x}} + (1.45 \text{ N})\,\mathbf{y}$.

$F_3 = \sqrt{(1.99 \text{ N})^2 + (1.45 \text{ N})^2} = \boxed{2.5 \text{ N}}$. $\theta = \tan^{-1}\left(\dfrac{1.45 \text{ N}}{1.99 \text{ N}}\right) = \boxed{36° \text{ above the } +x \text{ axis}}$.

22.   From Newton's second law, $\Sigma F = ma$,

we have $a = \dfrac{\Sigma F}{m} = \dfrac{3.0 \text{ N}}{1.5 \text{ kg}} = \boxed{2.0 \text{ m/s}^2 \text{ in the direction of the net force}}$.

30. $150 \text{ lb} = (150 \text{ lb}) \times \dfrac{4.45 \text{ N}}{1 \text{ lb}} = \boxed{668 \text{ N}}$.   From $w = mg$,

we have $m = \dfrac{w}{g} = \dfrac{668 \text{ N}}{9.80 \text{ m/s}^2} = \boxed{68.2 \text{ kg}}$.

34.   The resistive force is opposite the forward force. From Newton's second law, $\Sigma F = ma$,

we have $a = \dfrac{\Sigma F}{m} = \dfrac{15 \text{ N} - 8.0 \text{ N}}{1.0 \text{ kg}} = \boxed{7.0 \text{ m/s}^2}$.

37   (a) From Newton's second law, $\Sigma F = ma$,

we have $a = \dfrac{\Sigma F}{m} = \dfrac{200\ \text{N} + 300\ \text{N} - 300\ \text{N}}{1500\ \text{kg}} = \boxed{0.133\ \text{m/s}^2}$.

(b) Once the car is moving, ΣF will be zero for constant velocity (a is zero).

So $\Sigma F = F - 300\ \text{N} = 0$. Therefore, $F = \boxed{300\ \text{N}}$.

38   We first find acceleration from kinematics. $v_0 = 90\ \text{km/h} = 25\ \text{m/s}$, $v = 0$, $t = 5.5\ \text{s}$.

From $v = v_0 + at$, we have $a = \dfrac{v - v_0}{t} = \dfrac{0 - 25\ \text{m/s}}{5.5\ \text{s}} = -4.56\ \text{m/s}^2$.

Using Newton's second law, $\Sigma F = ma = (60\ \text{kg})(-4.55\ \text{m/s}^2) = -\boxed{2.7 \times 10^2\ \text{N}}$.

The negative sign indicates that the force is opposite the motion or the velocity.

44.   (d). The action and reaction forces are equal, opposite, and on different objects.

49.   From Newton's second law, the force on the female by the male is

$F = ma = (45\ \text{kg})(2.0\ \text{m/s}^2) = 90\ \text{N}$.

The force on the male by the female is then also 90 N according to Newton's third law,

so $a_{\text{male}} = \dfrac{90\ \text{N}}{60\ \text{kg}} = \boxed{1.5\ \text{m/s}^2}$ opposite hers.

54.   (a) The scale reading is equal to the normal force on the person. We choose upward as positive.

Since $\Sigma F = w - N = ma = 0$, $N = w = mg = (75.0\ \text{kg})(9.80\ \text{m/s}^2) = \boxed{735\ \text{N}}$.

(b) a is still zero, so $N = \boxed{735\ \text{N}}$.

(c) From $\Sigma F = N - w = ma$,

$N = w + ma = mg + ma = m(g + a) = (75.0\ \text{kg})(9.80\ \text{m/s}^2 + 2.00\ \text{m/s}^2) = \boxed{885\ \text{N}}$.

58.   (a) Since $\Sigma F_x = F\cos 30° = (25\ \text{N})\cos 30° = 21.65\ \text{N} = ma_x$,

$a_x = \dfrac{21.65\ \text{N}}{30\ \text{kg}} = \boxed{0.72\ \text{m/s}^2}$.

(b) Also, $\Sigma F_y = N + F\sin 30° - w = ma_y = 0$,

$N = w - F\sin 30° = (30\ \text{kg})(9.80\ \text{m/s}^2) - (25\ \text{N})\sin 30° = \boxed{2.8 \times 10^2\ \text{N}}$.

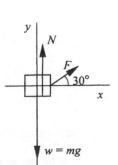

60. (a) There are $\boxed{\text{two}}$ forces acting on the skier, the weight of the skier and the normal force on the skier by the incline.

(b) The x-component of the weight is the side opposite the angle θ shown, so the sine function is used:

$$\Sigma F_x = mg \sin \theta = ma_x,\ a_x = g \sin \theta = (9.80\ \text{m/s}^2) \sin 37° = \boxed{5.9\ \text{m/s}^2}.$$

(c) We take $x_o = 0$. Since $v^2 = v_o^2 + 2a(x - x_o)$, $v = \sqrt{(5.0\ \text{m/s})^2 + 2(5.9\ \text{m/s}^2)(35\ \text{m})} = \boxed{21\ \text{m/s}}$.

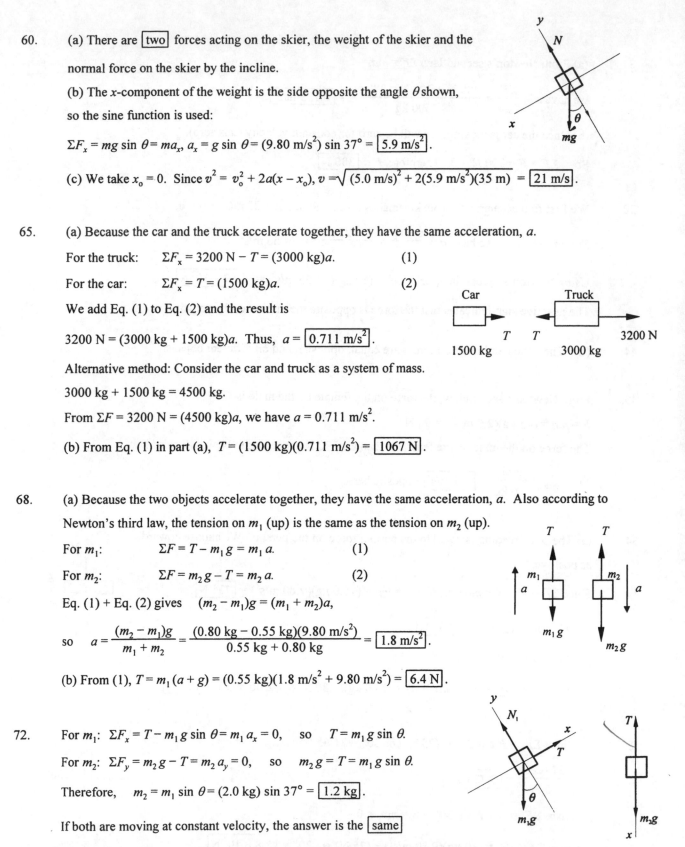

65. (a) Because the car and the truck accelerate together, they have the same acceleration, a.

For the truck: $\Sigma F_x = 3200\ \text{N} - T = (3000\ \text{kg})a.$ (1)

For the car: $\Sigma F_x = T = (1500\ \text{kg})a.$ (2)

We add Eq. (1) to Eq. (2) and the result is

$3200\ \text{N} = (3000\ \text{kg} + 1500\ \text{kg})a.$ Thus, $a = \boxed{0.711\ \text{m/s}^2}$.

Alternative method: Consider the car and truck as a system of mass.

$3000\ \text{kg} + 1500\ \text{kg} = 4500\ \text{kg}.$

From $\Sigma F = 3200\ \text{N} = (4500\ \text{kg})a$, we have $a = 0.711\ \text{m/s}^2$.

(b) From Eq. (1) in part (a), $T = (1500\ \text{kg})(0.711\ \text{m/s}^2) = \boxed{1067\ \text{N}}$.

68. (a) Because the two objects accelerate together, they have the same acceleration, a. Also according to Newton's third law, the tension on m_1 (up) is the same as the tension on m_2 (up).

For m_1: $\Sigma F = T - m_1 g = m_1 a.$ (1)

For m_2: $\Sigma F = m_2 g - T = m_2 a.$ (2)

Eq. (1) + Eq. (2) gives $(m_2 - m_1)g = (m_1 + m_2)a,$

so $a = \dfrac{(m_2 - m_1)g}{m_1 + m_2} = \dfrac{(0.80\ \text{kg} - 0.55\ \text{kg})(9.80\ \text{m/s}^2)}{0.55\ \text{kg} + 0.80\ \text{kg}} = \boxed{1.8\ \text{m/s}^2}.$

(b) From (1), $T = m_1 (a + g) = (0.55\ \text{kg})(1.8\ \text{m/s}^2 + 9.80\ \text{m/s}^2) = \boxed{6.4\ \text{N}}$.

72. For m_1: $\Sigma F_x = T - m_1 g \sin \theta = m_1 a_x = 0,$ so $T = m_1 g \sin \theta.$

For m_2: $\Sigma F_y = m_2 g - T = m_2 a_y = 0,$ so $m_2 g = T = m_1 g \sin \theta.$

Therefore, $m_2 = m_1 \sin \theta = (2.0\ \text{kg}) \sin 37° = \boxed{1.2\ \text{kg}}.$

If both are moving at constant velocity, the answer is the $\boxed{\text{same}}$

1.2 kg, because the acceleration is still zero and the forces must still balance out.

76. (c). The coefficient of kinetic friction, μ_k, is usually smaller than μ_s.

82. (a) From $\Sigma F_y = N - mg = ma_y = 0$, we have $N = mg$.

Also, $\Sigma F_x = F - f_s = ma_x = 0$ (on the verge of moving),

so $f_{s_{max}} = \mu_s N = F$, or $\mu_s = \dfrac{F}{mg} = \dfrac{275 \text{ N}}{(35.0 \text{ kg})(9.80 \text{ m/s}^2)} = \boxed{0.802}$.

(b) Similarly, $\mu_k = \dfrac{195 \text{ N}}{(35.0 \text{ kg})(9.80 \text{ m/s}^2)} = \boxed{0.569}$.

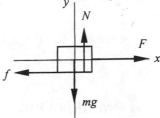

85. From $\Sigma F_y = N - mg = ma_y = 0$, we have $N = mg$.

$f_{s_{max}} = \mu_s N = \mu_s mg = 0.60(50 \text{ kg})(9.80 \text{ m/s}^2) = 294 \text{ N}$.

$f_k = \mu_k mg = 0.40(50 \text{ kg})(9.80 \text{ m/s}^2) = 196 \text{ N}$.

(a) Since $250 \text{ N} < f_{s_{max}} = 294 \text{ N}$, the object won't move,

so $a = \boxed{0}$.

(b) Since $350 > f_{s_{max}} = 294 \text{ N}$, the object will move, and f_k must used.

$\Sigma F_x = 350 \text{ N} - 196 \text{ N} = 154 \text{ N} = ma = (50 \text{ kg})a$.

Thus, $a = \boxed{3.1 \text{ m/s}^2}$.

86. (a) We first find acceleration from dynamics and use μ_k from Table 4.1.

From $\Sigma F_x = -f_k = -\mu_k mg = ma$, we have $\mu_k = -\dfrac{a}{g}$,

so $a = -\mu_k g = -0.85(9.80 \text{ m/s}^2) = -8.33 \text{ m/s}^2$,

and $v_0 = 90 \text{ km/h} = 25 \text{ m/s}$, $v = 0$. (Taking $x_0 = 0$.)

Since $v^2 = v_0^2 + 2a(x - x_0)$, $x = \dfrac{v^2 - v_0^2}{2a} = \dfrac{0 - (25 \text{ m/s})^2}{2(-8.33 \text{ m/s}^2)} = \boxed{38 \text{ m}}$.

(b) $a = -0.60(9.80 \text{ m/s}^2) = -5.88 \text{ m/s}^2$, so $x = \dfrac{0 - (25 \text{ m/s})^2}{2(-5.88 \text{ m/s}^2)} = \boxed{53 \text{ m}}$.

90. $\boxed{\text{Yes}}$, the coefficient of kinetic friction can be found.

From $\Sigma F_y = N - mg \cos \theta = ma_y = 0$, we have $N = mg \cos \theta$.

For constant velocity, $a_x = 0$, so $\Sigma F_x = mg \sin \theta - f_k = 0$,

or $mg \sin \theta = \mu_k N = \mu_k (mg \cos \theta)$.

Therefore, $\mu_k = \dfrac{\sin \theta}{\cos \theta} = \boxed{\tan \theta}$.

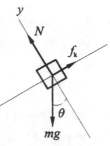

101. We first find the acceleration from kinematics.

Given: $x = 0.750$ m, $v_o = 0$, $v = 300$ m/s. Find: a. (Taking $x_o = 0$.)

From $v^2 = v_o^2 + 2a(x - x_o)$, we have $a = \dfrac{(300 \text{ m/s})^2 - (0)^2}{2(0.750 \text{ m})} = 6.0 \times 10^4 \text{ m/s}^2$.

Then, $F = ma = (0.0250 \text{ kg})(6.0 \times 10^4 \text{ m/s}^2) = \boxed{1.5 \times 10^3 \text{ N}}$.

109. We first find acceleration from dynamics. From the result of Exercise 4.86(a), $\mu_k = -\dfrac{a}{g}$,

so $a = -\mu_k g = -(0.20)((9.80 \text{ m/s}^2) = -1.96 \text{ m/s}^2$.

Now, given: $v_o = 4.5$ m/s, $v = 0$, $a = -1.96$ m/s^2. Find: x. (Taking $x_o = 0$.)

From $v^2 = 0 = v_o^2 + 2a(x - x_o)$, we have $x = -\dfrac{v_o^2}{2a} = -\dfrac{(4.5 \text{ m/s})^2}{2(-1.96 \text{ m/s}^2)} = \boxed{5.2 \text{ m}}$.

V. Practice Quiz

1. Which of Newton's laws of motion *best* explains why motorists should buckle up?

   (a) the first law   (b) the second law   (c) the third law   (d) the law of gravitation

2. A net force F accelerates a mass m with an acceleration a. If the same net force is applied to mass $m/2$, then the acceleration will be

   (a) $4a$.   (b) $2a$.   (c) a.   (d) $a/2$.   (e) $a/4$.

3. A brick hits a window and breaks the glass. Because the brick breaks the glass,

   (a) the force on the brick is greater in magnitude than the force on the glass.

   (b) the force on the brick is smaller in magnitude than the force on the glass.

   (c) the force on the brick is equal in magnitude to the force on the glass.

   (d) the force on the brick is in the same direction as the force on the glass.

   (e) the brick did not slow down.

4. An object weighs 100 N on the surface of Earth. What is the mass of this object on the surface of the Moon where the acceleration due to gravity is only 1/6 of that on the Earth?

   (a) 1.70 kg   (b) 10.2 kg   (c) 16.7 kg   (d) 58.8 kg   (e) 100 kg

5. Two horizontal forces act on a 5.0-kg object. One force has a magnitude of 8.0 N and is directed due north. The second force has a magnitude of 6.0 N toward the east. What is the acceleration of the object?

   (a) 1.6 m/s^2 north   (b) 1.2 m/s^2 east   (c) 2.0 m/s^2 at 53° north of east   (d) 2.0 m/s^2 at 53° east of north

6. A box is placed on a smooth inclined plane with an angle of 20° to the horizontal. If the inclined plane is 5.0 m long, how long does it take for the mass to reach the bottom of the inclined plane after the mass is released from rest?

(a) 1.0 s   (b) 1.3 s   (c) 1.5 s   (d) 1.7 s   (e) 1.9 s

7. During a hockey game, a hockey puck is given an initial speed of 10 m/s. It slides 50 m on the ice before it stops. What is the coefficient of kinetic friction between the puck and the ice?

(a) 0.090   (b) 0.10   (c) 0.11   (d) 0.12   (e) 0.13

8. A person on a scale rides in an elevator. If the mass of the person is 60 kg and the elevator accelerates upward with an acceleration of 4.9 m/s^2, what is the reading on the scale in newtons?

(a) 147 N   (b) 294 N   (c) 588 N   (d) 882 N   (e) 1176 N

9. A traffic light of weight 100 N is supported by two ropes as shown in the diagram. What are the tensions in the ropes?

(a) 50 N   (b) 63 N   (c) 66 N   (d) 83 N   (e) 100 N

10. A crate is on a 20° inclined plane where the coefficients of static and kinetic friction is 0.45 and 0.35, respectively. What is the acceleration of the crate?

(a) zero   (b) 3.4 m/s^2 (c) 3.6 m/s^2 (d) 4.4 m/s^2 (e) 9.2 m/s^2

11. Find the magnitudes of the acceleration of the system and the tension in the connecting string. (Neglect friction and mass of the pulley.)

(a) 5.3 m/s^2, 7.5 N   (b) 4.5 m/s^2, 7.1 N   (c) 0.89 m/s^2, 5.3 N
(d) 0.090 m/s^2, 4.9 N   (e) 1.2 m/s^2, 4.3 N.

12. The engine of a small plane of mass 2.00×10^3 kg can supply a forward thrust force of 1.50×10^4 N. How long a runway is required if the takeoff speed of the plane is 45.0 m/s?

(a) 6.00 m   (b) 34.4 m/s^2 (c) 135 m   (d) 207 m   (e) 338 m

Answers to Practice Quiz:

1. a   2. b   3. c   4. b   5. c   6. d   7. b   8. d   9. d   10. a   11. c   12. c

CHAPTER 5

Work and Energy

I.   Chapter Objectives

Upon completion of this chapter, you should be able to:

1.   define mechanical work and compute the work done in various situations.

2.   differentiate between work done by constant and variable forces and compute the work done by a spring force.

3.   study the work–energy theorem and apply it in solving problems.

4.   define and understand potential energy and learn about gravitational potential energy.

5.   distinguish between conservative and nonconservative forces and explain their effects on the conservation of energy.

6.   define power and describe mechanical efficiency.

II.   Chapter Summary and Discussion

1.   Work Done by a Constant Force (Section 5.1)

The **work** done by a constant force is $W = (F \cos \theta) d$, where F and d are the magnitudes of the force and displacement vectors, respectively, and θ is the angle between these two vectors. Although force and displacement are vectors, work is a scalar quantity. Work can be either positive or negative, depending on the angle θ between the force vector and the displacement vector. If $0° \leq \theta < 90°$, work is positive; if $90° < \theta \leq 180°$, work is negative; if $\theta = 90°$, work is equal to zero. The SI unit of work is N·m, which is called a joule (J).

Note: The angle in the work definition is the *angle between the force vector and the displacement vector*, which is not necessarily the angle from the horizontal.

Graphically, the work done by a force is equal to the area under the curve in a force-versus-position graph.

Example 5.1   A 500-kg elevator is pulled upward by a constant force of 5500 N for a distance of 50.0 m.

(a) Find the work done by the upward force.

(b) Find the work done by the gravitational force.

(c) Find the work done by the net force (the net work done on the elevator).

Solution: Given: $F_{up} = 5500$ N, $w = mg = (500\ \text{kg})(9.80\ \text{m/s}^2) = 4900$ N, $d = 50.0$ m.

Find: (a) W_{up}, (b) W_{grav}, and (c) W_{net}.

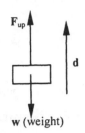

(a) The displacement is upward and the upward force is (of course) upward, so the angle between them is zero.

Therefore, $W_{up} = (F \cos \theta)\, d = (F_{up} \cos 0°)\, d = (5500\ \text{N})(1)(50.0\ \text{m}) = 2.75 \times 10^5$ J.

(b) The displacement is upward and the gravitational force (weight) is downward, so the angle between them is 180°.

Therefore, $W_{grav} = (w \cos 180°)\, d = (4900\ \text{N})(-1)(50.0\ \text{m}) = -2.45 \times 10^5$ J.

(c) The work done by the net force is equal to the net work done on the elevator.

$W_{net} = W_{up} + W_{grav} = 2.75 \times 10^5\ \text{J} + (-2.45 \times 10^5\ \text{J}) = 3.0 \times 10^4$ J.

Note: W_{net} is also equal to $W_{net} = (F_{net} \cos \theta)\, d$, where $F_{net} = F - w$.

$F_{net} = 5500\ \text{N} - 4900\ \text{N} = 600$ N.

$W_{net} = (600\text{N}) \cos 0°\, (50.0\ \text{m}) = 3.0 \times 10^4$ J.

Example 5.2 A force moves an object in the direction of the force. The graph shows the force versus the object's position. Find the net work done when the object moves

(a) from 0 to 2.0 m.

(b) from 2.0 to 4.0 m.

(c) from 4.0 to 6.0 m.

(d) from 0 to 6.0 m.

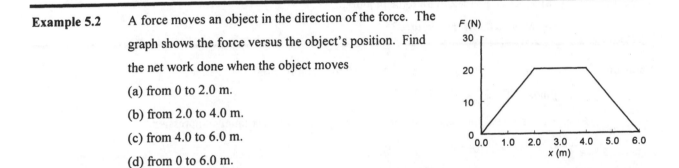

Solution:

Work done is equal to the area under the curve.

(a) The area under the curve from 0 to 2.0 m is the left triangle. The area of a triangle is $\frac{1}{2}(\text{base} \times \text{height})$,

so $W_{0-2} = \frac{1}{2}(2.0\ \text{m} - 0)(20\ \text{N}) = 20$ J.

(b) The area under the curve from 2.0 m to 4.0 m is the rectangle,

so $W_{2-4} = (4.0\ \text{m} - 2.0\ \text{m})(20\ \text{N}) = 40$ J.

(c) The area under the curve from 4.0 m to 6.0 m is the right triangle,

so $W_{4-6} = \frac{1}{2}(6.0\ \text{m} - 4.0\ \text{m})(20\ \text{N}) = 20$ J.

(d) The area under the curve from 0 to 6.0 m is the sum of the areas of the two triangles and the rectangle.

Thus, $W_{0-6} = W_{0-2} + W_{2-4} + W_{4-6} = 20\ \text{J} + 40\ \text{J} + 20\ \text{J} = 80$ J.

---

2. Work Done by a Variable Force (Section 5.2)

Our discussion of variable force in this section is restricted to spring force described by Hooke's law, $F_s = -kx$ (with $x_o = 0$), where k is a constant called the *spring constant* or *force constant* that measures the stiffness of a spring, x is the displacement from the spring's unstretched position (x_o), and the negative sign indicates that the spring force and the spring displacement are always opposite each other. Hooke's law is a linear equation; that is, doubling x will also double F_s.

The work done by an external force in stretching or compressing a spring (overcoming the spring force) is $W = \frac{1}{2}kx^2$, where x is the stretch or compression distance. Note that this expression is a quadratic expression; that is, doubling x will quadruple W.

Example 5.3   A spring of spring constant 20 N/m is to be compressed by 0.10 m.

   (a) What is the maximum force required?

   (b) What is the work required?

Solution: Given: $k = 20$ N/m   and $x = -0.10$ m (compression).

   Find: (a) $F_{s_{max}}$ (b) W.

   (a) From Hooke's law, the maximum force corresponds to the maximum compression.

   $F_{s_{max}} = -kx = -(20 \text{ N/m})(-0.10 \text{ m}) = 2.0$ N.

   (b) $W = \frac{1}{2}kx^2 = \frac{1}{2}(20 \text{ N/m})(-0.10 \text{ m})^2 = 0.10$ J.

---

3. The Work-Energy Theorem: Kinetic Energy (Section 5.3)

Kinetic energy is the energy of motion, and it is defined as $K = \frac{1}{2}mv^2$, where m is the mass and v is the velocity of the object. Although velocity is a vector quantity, kinetic energy is a scalar quantity because it depends on the square of velocity. The SI unit of kinetic energy is the joule (J).

By combining the definition of work, a kinematic equation, and Newton's second law, we can derive the **work–energy theorem**, which states that the net work done on an object is equal to its change in kinetic energy, i.e., $W_{net} = K - K_o = \Delta K$. In general, work is a measure of energy transfer, and energy is the capacity to do work.

Example 5.4   An object hits a wall and bounces back with half of its original speed. What is the ratio of the final kinetic energy to the initial kinetic energy?

Solution: Given: $v = \dfrac{v_0}{2}$.   Find: $\dfrac{K}{K_0}$.

$K_0 = \frac{1}{2}mv_0^2$ and $K = \frac{1}{2}mv^2 = \frac{1}{2}m\left(\dfrac{v_0}{2}\right)^2 = \frac{1}{4}\left(\frac{1}{2}m v_0^2\right)$.   So $\dfrac{K}{K_0} = \frac{1}{4}$.

Why isn't the result $\frac{1}{2}$?

Because the work–energy theorem is a combination of kinematics and dynamics, it offers a convenient method for solving mechanical problems. Rather than working from kinematics then to dynamics or vice versa, we can use this new theorem to solve these typical "two-step" problems in a single step, as the following example shows.

Example 5.5   The kinetic friction force between a 60.0-kg object and a horizontal surface is 50.0 N. If the initial speed of the object is 25.0 m/s, what distance will it slide before coming to a stop?

Solution: Given: $m = 60.0$ kg, $v_0 = 25.0$ m/s, $v = 0$, $f_k = 50.0$ N.

Find: d.

The kinetic friction force f_k is the only unbalanced force, and the angle between the friction force and the displacement is 180°. With $W_{net} = K - K_0$, we have

$W_{net} = (F \cos \theta)\, d = (f_k \cos 180°)\, d = (50.0 \text{ N})(-1)d = K - K_0 = \frac{1}{2}mv^2 - \frac{1}{2}mv_0^2$

$= \frac{1}{2}(60.0 \text{ kg})(0)^2 - \frac{1}{2}(60.0 \text{ kg})(25.0 \text{ m/s})^2$.   Solving, we obtain $d = 3.75 \times 10^2$ m.

Note: This example can also be solved with dynamics and kinematics. We can first find the acceleration of the object from Newton's second law and then use kinematic equations to find the distance.

4.   Potential Energy (Section 5.4)

Potential energy is the energy of position. Two forms of potential energy are considered here, **gravitational potential energy** and **elastic (spring) potential energy**. A zero reference point/level is always required in measuring position and potential energy. For example, a question like, how high is that table? is really meaningless unless we specify a zero reference level such as the floor or the ground from which to measure that height. This choice of zero reference point/level is arbitrary, that is, you can choose anywhere as your zero reference point/level in your calculation, because what is important is the *change* in potential energy. With the zero potential location chosen as the zero reference point/level, the two forms of potential energy can be written as

Gravitational potential energy: $U = mgy$ (with $y_o = 0$)

Elastic potential energy: $U = \frac{1}{2}kx^2$ (with $x_o = 0$)

Example 5.6   A 10.0-kg object is moved from the second floor of a house 3.00 m above the ground to the first floor 0.30 m above the ground. What is the change in gravitational potential energy?

Solution: We choose the ground level as our reference level ($y_o = 0$).

Given: $m = 10.0$ kg, $y_1 = 3.00$ m, $y_2 = 0.30$ m.   Find: ΔU.

$\Delta U = U_2 - U_1 = mgy_2 - mgy_1 = mg(y_2 - y_1) = (10.0 \text{ kg})(9.80 \text{ m/s}^2)(0.30 \text{ m} - 3.00 \text{ m}) = -2.6 \times 10^2$ J.

As expected, ΔU is negative, since the object moves from a higher potential level to a lower potential level.

If we choose the reference level at the first-floor level (height is zero at that level), then

$y_1 = 3.00$ m - 0.30 m = 2.70, and $y_2 = 0$.

$\Delta U = mg(y_2 - y_1) = (10.0 \text{ kg})(9.80 \text{ m/s}^2)(0 - 2.70 \text{ m}) = -2.6 \times 10^2$ J, independent of reference choice.

Now, try to calculate the change in potential energy by choosing the second floor as the reference level.

Example 5.7   A spring with a spring constant of 15 N/m is initially compressed by 3.0 cm. How much work is required to compress the spring an additional 4.0 cm?

Solution: We choose the uncompressed position as $x_o = 0$.

Given: $k = 15$ N/m, $x_1 = 0.030$ m, $x_2 = x_1 + \Delta x = 0.030$ m + 0.040 m = 0.070 m.

Find: W.

The work required goes into the change in elastic potential energy: $W = \Delta K + \Delta U = \Delta U (\Delta K = 0)$.

$W = \Delta U = U_2 - U_1 = \frac{1}{2}kx_2^2 - \frac{1}{2}kx_1^2 = \frac{1}{2}k(x_2^2 - x_1^2) = \frac{1}{2}(15 \text{ N/m})[(0.070 \text{ m})^2 - (0.030 \text{ m})^2] = 0.030$ J.

Note: Why does $W \neq \frac{1}{2}k(x_2 - x_1)^2 = \frac{1}{2}(14 \text{ m/s})(0.070 \text{ m} - 0.030 \text{ m})^2 = 0.012$ J?

---

5.   The Conservation of Energy (Section 5.5)

A force is **conservative** if the work done by or against the force is independent of the path but dependent on only the initial and final locations. Gravitational force is an example of a conservative force. A force is **nonconservative** if the work done by or against it depends on the path. Force of friction is an example of a nonconservative force.

The **total mechanical energy** E of a system is defined as the sum of the kinetic energy and potential energy: $E = K + U$. If the working forces (the forces that are doing nonzero work) in a system are conservative, the total mechanical energy of the system is conserved. This is the principle of **conservation of total mechanical energy**:

$$K_o + U_o = K + U \quad \text{or} \quad \tfrac{1}{2}mv^2 + U = \tfrac{1}{2}mv_o^2 + U_o.$$

Note: When applying the principle of conservation of mechanical energy, you should choose a zero reference point/level from which to determine U-values. The choice is arbitrary, that is, you can choose the zero reference point/level to be anywhere it is convenient. Also, clearly identify the initial and final velocities, and the initial and final positions. These are the only four physical quantities involved in mechanical energy conservation, so you need to know three of them before you can solve the problem.

Example 5.8   A 70-kg skier starts from rest on top of a 25-m-high slope. What is the speed of the skier at the bottom of the slope? (Neglect friction.)

Solution: We choose the bottom of the slope as the zero reference level ($y = 0$).

Given: $v_o = 0$, $y_o = 25$ m, $y = 0$.

Find: v.

$v_o = 0, y_o = 25$ m

25 m

Reference level $y = 0, v = ?$

From the conservation of mechanical energy,

$$K_o + U_o = K + U \quad \text{or} \quad \tfrac{1}{2}mv^2 + U = \tfrac{1}{2}mv_o^2 + U_o,$$

we have $\tfrac{1}{2}mv^2 + mgy = \tfrac{1}{2}mv_o^2 + mgy_o.$

Thus, $\tfrac{1}{2}mv^2 + mg(0) = \tfrac{1}{2}m(0)^2 + mgy_o,$ or $\tfrac{1}{2}mv^2 = mgy_o.$

Therefore, $v = \sqrt{2gh_o} = \sqrt{2(9.80 \text{ m/s}^2)(25 \text{ m})} = 22$ m/s.

Note: We did not even use the mass of the skier! (The mass of the skier cancels out in the equation.)

Example 5.9   A 1500-kg car moving at 25 m/s hits an initially uncompressed horizontal spring with a spring constant of 2.0×10^6 N/m. What is the maximum compression of the spring? (Neglect the mass of the spring.)

Solution: Given: $m = 1500$ kg, $k = 2.0 \times 10^6$ N/m, $v_o = 25$ m/s, $v = 0$, $x_o = 0$.

(Remember, we need three known velocity and/or position quantities.)

Find: x.

Here we choose the uncompressed position of the spring as the reference point ($x_o = 0$). Before the car hits the spring, the car is moving with an initial speed of 25 m/s, and the compression of the spring is zero. When the spring is maximally compressed, the car stops (transfer all its kinetic energy to elastic potential energy in the spring) and the spring is compressed by a distance x. From the conservation of mechanical energy, $K_o + U_o = K + U$ or $\frac{1}{2}mv^2 + U = \frac{1}{2}mv_o^2 + U_o$,

we have $\frac{1}{2}mv^2 + \frac{1}{2}kx^2 = \frac{1}{2}mv_o^2 + \frac{1}{2}kx_o^2$.

Thus, $\frac{1}{2}m(0) + \frac{1}{2}kx^2 = \frac{1}{2}mv_o^2 + \frac{1}{2}k(0)^2$, or $\frac{1}{2}kx^2 = \frac{1}{2}mv_o^2$.

Therefore, $x = \sqrt{\dfrac{mv_o^2}{k}} = \sqrt{\dfrac{m}{k}}\, v_o = \sqrt{\dfrac{1500 \text{ kg}}{2.0 \times 10^6 \text{ N/m}}}\ (25 \text{ m/s}) = 0.68$ m.

If there is a nonconservative force doing nonzero work in a system, the total mechanical energy of the system is *not* conserved; however, the total energy (not mechanical!) of the system is still conserved. Some of the energy is used to overcome the work done by the nonconservative force. The difference in mechanical energy is equal to the work done by the nonconservative force, that is, $W_{nc} = E_o - E = -\Delta E$.

Example 5.10   In Example 5.8, if the work done by the kinetic friction force is -6.0×10^3 J (the work done by kinetic friction force is negative because the angle between the friction force and the displacement is 180°), what is the speed of the skier at the bottom of the slope?

Solution:

Because the kinetic friction force is a nonconservative force, mechanical energy is *not* conserved; however, the difference in mechanical energy is equal to the work done by the friction force:

$W_{nc} = E - E_o = (\frac{1}{2}mv^2 + mgy) - (\frac{1}{2}mv_o^2 + mgy_o)$.

Thus, -6.0×10^3 J $= \frac{1}{2}(70 \text{ kg})v^2 + mg(0) - \frac{1}{2}m\,(0)^2 - (70 \text{ kg})(9.80 \text{ m/s}^2)(25 \text{ m})$,

and $v = 18$ m/s.

---

6.   Power (Section 5.6)

Average **power** is the average rate of doing work (work done divided by time interval), $\overline{P} = \dfrac{W}{t}$. The SI unit of power is the watt (W). A common British unit of power is horsepower (hp), and 1 hp = 746 W. If the work is done by a constant force in the direction of motion or displacement ($\theta = 0°$), and the object is moved through a distance d, $\overline{P} = \dfrac{Fd}{t} = F\,\overline{v}$, where $\dfrac{d}{t} = \overline{v}$ is the magnitude of the average velocity.

Example 5.11   A 1500-kg car accelerates from 0 to 25 m/s in 7.0 s. What is the average power delivered to the car by the engine? Ignore all frictional and other losses.

Solution: Given: $m = 1500$ kg, $v_0 = 0$, $v = 25$ m/s, $t = 7.0$ s.   Find: $\overline{P}$.

Because power is the rate of doing work, we need to calculate the work done to the car first.

From the work-energy theorem, $W = \Delta K = \frac{1}{2}mv^2 - \frac{1}{2}mv_0^2 = \frac{1}{2}(1500 \text{ kg})[(25 \text{ m/s})^2 - (0)^2] = 4.69 \times 10^5$ J,

so $\overline{P} = \dfrac{W}{t} = \dfrac{4.69 \times 10^5 \text{ J}}{7.0 \text{ s}} = 6.7 \times 10^4$ W $= 90$ hp.

Alternative method: The average velocity of the car is $\overline{v} = \dfrac{v + v_0}{2} = \dfrac{25 \text{ m/s} + 0}{2} = 12.5$ m/s.

From Newton's second law, $F = ma = m\dfrac{v - v_0}{t} = (1500 \text{ kg}) \times \dfrac{25 \text{ m/s} - 0}{7.0 \text{ s}} = 5.36 \times 10^3$ N,

so $\overline{P} = F\,\overline{v} = (5.36 \times 10^3 \text{ N})(12.5 \text{ m/s}) = 6.7 \times 10^4$ W $= 90$ hp.

Mechanical efficiency is a measure of the useful work or power output compared with the energy or power input. **Efficiency** ε is defined as a fraction (or percentage):

$$\varepsilon = \frac{W_{\text{out}}}{W_{\text{in}}}\,(\times\,100\%) = \frac{P_{\text{out}}}{P_{\text{in}}}\,(\times\,100\%)$$

Efficiency is a unitless quantity.

III.   Mathematical Summary

Work by Constant Force	$W = (F\cos\theta)d$	(5.2)	Defines work done by a constant force.
Hooke's Law (spring force)	$F_s = -kx$	(5.3)	Relates spring force with spring constant and change in length ($x_0 = 0$)
Work done by a Spring Force	$W = \frac{1}{2}kx^2$	(5.4)	Relates work done by external force in stretching or compressing a spring.
Kinetic Energy	$K = \frac{1}{2}mv^2$	(5.5)	Defines kinetic energy in terms of mass and velocity.
Work-Energy Theorem	$W_{\text{net}} = K - K_0 = \Delta K$	(5.6)	The net work done on an object is equal to the change in kinetic energy.
Potential Energy of a Spring	$U = \frac{1}{2}kx^2$ (with $x_0 = 0$)	(5.7)	Defines elastic potential energy.
Gravitational Potential Energy	$U = mgy$ (with $y_0 = 0$)	(5.8)	Defines gravitational potential energy.

Conservation of Mechanical Energy	$\frac{1}{2}mv^2 + U = \frac{1}{2}mv_0^2 + U_0$ (5.10)	States that the total mechanical energy of a system is conserved if only conservative forces are doing work.
Nonconservative Force	$W_{nc} = E - E_0 = \Delta E$ (5.13)	Equates the work done by nonconservative force to the change in mechanical energy of a system.
Average Power	$\overline{P} = \dfrac{W}{t} = \dfrac{Fd}{t} = F\overline{v}$ (5.15)	Defines and calculates the average power delivered by a constant force in direction of d and v.
	$\overline{P} = \dfrac{Fd\cos\theta}{t}$ (5.16)	If the force makes an angle θ with d or v.
Efficiency (percent)	$\varepsilon = \dfrac{W_{out}}{W_{in}}\,(\times 100\%)$ (5.17)	Defines the mechanical efficiency of a system.
	$= \dfrac{P_{out}}{P_{in}}\,(\times 100\%)$ (5.18)	

IV. Solutions of Selected Exercises and Paired Exercises

8. From $W = F\cos\theta\, d$, we $F = \dfrac{W}{d\cos\theta} = \dfrac{50\ \text{J}}{(10\ \text{m})\cos 0°} = \boxed{5.0\ \text{N}}$.

15. (a) The weight does $\boxed{\text{negative}}$ work because its direction is opposite (180°) the displacement (up).

(b) When the balloon ascends at constant rate, the upward force is equal to its weight.

$W = F\cos\theta\, d = (mg)\cos\theta\, d = (500\ \text{kg})(9.80\ \text{m/s}^2)(\cos 0°)[(1.50\ \text{m/s})(20.0\ \text{s})] = \boxed{1.47 \times 10^5\ \text{J}}$.

16. $\Sigma F_y = N + F\sin\theta - mg = 0, \quad N = mg - F\sin\theta.$

$\Sigma F_x = F\cos\theta - f_k = 0, \quad \text{or} \quad F\cos\theta = \mu_k N = \mu_k(mg - F\sin\theta) = 0.$

Thus, $F = \dfrac{\mu_k mg}{\cos\theta + \mu_k \sin\theta} = \dfrac{0.20(35\ \text{kg})(9.80\ \text{m/s}^2)}{\cos 30° + 0.20\sin 30°} = 71.0\ \text{N}.$

Therefore, $W = F\cos\theta\, d = (71.0\ \text{N})\cos 30°\,(10\ \text{m}) = \boxed{6.1 \times 10^2\ \text{J}}$.

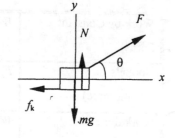

26. $W = \frac{1}{2}kx^2 = \frac{1}{2}(40\ \text{N/m})(0.020\ \text{m})^2 = \boxed{8.0 \times 10^{-3}\ \text{J}}$.

29. From $F_s = -kx$, we have $k = \left|\dfrac{F_s}{x_1 - x_0}\right| = \dfrac{(0.075\ \text{kg})(9.80\ \text{m/s}^2)}{0.070\ \text{m} - 0.040\ \text{m}} = 24.5\ \text{N/m}.$

The total stretch of the spring is $x = 0.10\ \text{m} + 0.030\ \text{m} = 0.13\ \text{m}$,

So $W = \frac{1}{2}kx^2 = \frac{1}{2}(24.5\ \text{N/m})(0.13\ \text{m})^2 = \boxed{0.21\ \text{J}}$.

30.   (a) $W = \frac{1}{2}kx^2 = \frac{1}{2}(2.5 \times 10^3 \text{ N/m})(0.060 \text{ m})^2 = \boxed{4.5 \text{ J}}$.

        (b) The difference in work is $\Delta W = \frac{1}{2}k(x_2^2 - x_1^2) = \frac{1}{2}(2.5 \times 10^3 \text{ N/m})[(0.080 \text{ m})^2 - (0.060 \text{ m})^2] = \boxed{3.5 \text{ J}}$.

36.   (a) $K = \frac{1}{2}mv^2 = \frac{1}{2}(4m)v^2 = 2mv^2$.   (b) $K = \frac{1}{2}(3m)(2v)^2 = 6mv^2$.

        (c) $K = \frac{1}{2}(2m)(3v)^2 = 9mv^2$.   (d) $K = \frac{1}{2}(m)(4v)^2 = 8mv^2$.

        Thus, the answer is (a).

39.   From the work-energy theorem, we have $W = \Delta K = \frac{1}{2}mv'^2 - \frac{1}{2}mv_0^2 = \frac{1}{2}mv'^2 - 0 = \frac{1}{2}mv'^2$,

        so $v = \sqrt{\dfrac{2W}{m}}$.   Therefore, $\dfrac{v'}{v} = \sqrt{\dfrac{W'}{W}} = \sqrt{\dfrac{2W}{W}} = \sqrt{2}$.

        Thus, $v' = \boxed{\sqrt{2}v}$.

42.   90 km/h = 25 m/s.

        (a) $K_0 = \frac{1}{2}mv_0^2 = \frac{1}{2}(1.2 \times 10^3 \text{ kg})(25 \text{ m/s})^2 = \boxed{3.8 \times 10^5 \text{ J}}$.

        (b) From the work-energy theorem, $W_{net} = \frac{1}{2}mv^2 - \frac{1}{2}mv_0^2 = 0 - 3.8 \times 10^5 \text{ J} = \boxed{-3.8 \times 10^5 \text{ J}}$.

55.   We first find the maximum height from kinematics.   (Take $y_0 = 0$.)

        From $v^2 = 0^2 = v_0^2 - 2g(y - y_0)$, we have $y_{max} = \dfrac{v_0^2}{2g} = \dfrac{(7.5 \text{ m/s})^2}{2(9.80 \text{ m/s}^2)} = 2.87 \text{ m}$.

        (a) $U = mgy = (0.20 \text{ kg})(9.80 \text{ m/s}^2)(1.2 \text{ m} + 2.87 \text{ m}) = \boxed{8.0 \text{ J}}$.

        (b) $\Delta U = mg\,\Delta y = (0.20 \text{ kg})(9.80 \text{ m/s}^2)(2.87 \text{ m}) = \boxed{5.6 \text{ J}}$.

56.   (a) On the board: $U = mgy = (60 \text{ kg})(9.80 \text{ m/s}^2)(5.0 \text{ m}) = \boxed{2.9 \times 10^3 \text{ J}}$.

        At the bottom of the pool: $U = (60 \text{ kg})(9.80 \text{ m/s}^2)(-3.0 \text{ m}) = \boxed{-1.8 \times 10^3 \text{ J}}$.

        (b) To the board: $\Delta U = mg\,\Delta y = (60 \text{ kg})(9.80 \text{ m/s}^2)(-8.0 \text{ m} - 0) = \boxed{-4.7 \times 10^3 \text{ J}}$.

        To the surface: $\Delta U = (60 \text{ kg})(9.80 \text{ m/s}^2)(-3.0 \text{ m} - 5.0 \text{ m}) = \boxed{-4.7 \times 10^3 \text{ J}}$.

        To the bottom of the pool: $\Delta U = (60 \text{ kg})(9.80 \text{ m/s}^2)(0 - 8.0 \text{ m}) = \boxed{-4.7 \times 10^3 \text{ J}}$.

66.   (a) $E_o = K_o + U_o = 0 + (0.250 \text{ kg})(9.80 \text{ m/s}^2)(115 \text{ m}) = \boxed{282 \text{ J}}$.

        (b) $U_1 = (0.250 \text{ kg})(9.80 \text{ m/s}^2)(115 \text{ m} - 75.0 \text{ m}) = \boxed{98.0 \text{ J}}$.

        Because $E = E_o$ is conserved, $K_1 = E_o - U_1 = 282 \text{ J} - 98.0 \text{ J} = \boxed{184 \text{ J}}$.

        (c) $E_2 = K_2 + 0 = \boxed{282 \text{ J}}$.   Because $K_2 = \frac{1}{2}mv^2$, $v = \sqrt{\dfrac{2K_2}{m}} = \sqrt{\dfrac{2(282 \text{ J})}{0.250 \text{ kg}}} = \boxed{47.5 \text{ m/s}}$.

        (d) For (a) $E_o = 0 + 0 = \boxed{0}$.

        For (b) $U_1 = (0.250 \text{ kg})(9.80 \text{ m/s}^2)(-75.0 \text{ m}) = \boxed{-184 \text{ J}}$. $K_1 = 0 - (-184 \text{ J}) = \boxed{184 \text{ J}}$.

        For (c) $E_2 = K_2 + U_2 = \boxed{0}$. $K_2 = 0 - (0.250 \text{ kg})(9.80 \text{ m/s}^2)(-115 \text{ m}) = 282 \text{ J}$.

        Thus, $v = \sqrt{\dfrac{2(282 \text{ J})}{0.250 \text{ kg}}} = \boxed{47.5 \text{ m/s}}$.

69.   (a) The mechanical energy ($E = K + U$) is 80 J. From the conservation of energy, the potential energy at the maximum height is 80 J because the kinetic energy is zero there. At three-fourths of the distance to the maximum height, the potential energy is

        $U = \frac{3}{4}(80 \text{ J}) = 60 \text{ J}$,   so $K = 80 \text{ J} - 60 \text{ J} = \boxed{20 \text{ J}}$; $U = \boxed{60 \text{ J}}$.

        (b) From $K = \frac{1}{2}mv^2$, we have $v = \sqrt{\dfrac{2K}{m}} = \sqrt{\dfrac{2(20 \text{ J})}{0.50 \text{ kg}}} = \boxed{8.9 \text{ m/s}}$.

        (c) The kinetic energy is zero at the maximum height, so $U = \boxed{80 \text{ J}}$.

72.   We choose the bottom of the slope (point B) as the reference for height ($y_o = 0$).

        From the conservation of mechanical energy, $\frac{1}{2}mv_B^2 + U_B = \frac{1}{2}mv_A^2 + U_A$,

        we have $\frac{1}{2}mv_B^2 + mg(0) = \frac{1}{2}m(5.0 \text{ m/s})^2 + mg\,(10 \text{ m})$.

        Solving, we obtain $v_B = \sqrt{(5.0 \text{ m/s})^2 + 2(9.80 \text{ m/s}^2)(10 \text{ m})} = \boxed{15 \text{ m/s}}$.

86.   90 km/h = 25 m/s.

        We can find the work from the work-energy theorem, $W = \Delta K = \frac{1}{2}mv^2 - 0 = \frac{1}{2}mv^2$.

        Thus, the average power is $\overline{P} = \dfrac{W}{t} = \dfrac{mv^2}{2t} = \dfrac{(1500 \text{ kg})(25 \text{ m/s})^2}{2(5.0 \text{ s})} = \boxed{9.4 \times 10^4 \text{ W} = 1.3 \times 10^2 \text{ hp}}$.

89. $P = (0.45)(2.0 \text{ hp})(746 \text{ W/hp}) = 6.7 \times 10^2 \text{ W} = 6.7 \times 10^2 \text{ J/s}$.

        In one second the energy is then $(6.7 \times 10^2 \text{ J/s})(1 \text{ s}) = \boxed{6.7 \times 10^2 \text{ J}}$.

101.   (a) 20.0×0.278 m/s = 5.56 m/s.   The power is $P = Fv = (700$ N$)(5.556$ m/s$) = 3892$ W,

so the work is $W = Pt = (3892$ W$)(3.50$ min$)(60$ s/min$) = \boxed{8.17 \times 10^5 \text{ J}}$.

(b) As in (a), $P = \boxed{3.90 \times 10^3 \text{ W}}$.

V.   Practice Quiz

1.   Which one of the following is the correct unit of work expressed in SI base units?

(a) kg·m/s   (b) kg·m/s^2 (c) kg·m^2/s   (d) kg·m^2/s^2 (e) kg^2·m/s^2

2.   A 40-N crate is pulled 5.0 m up along a 37° inclined plane. What is the magnitude of the work done by the weight (gravitational force) of the crate? (*Hint*: Draw a diagram.)

(a) 6.0 J   (b) 12 J   (c) 1.2×10^2 J   (d) 2.0×10^2 J   (e) 1.2×10^3 J.

3.   What work is required to stretch a spring of spring constant 40 N/m from $x = 0.20$ m to 0.25 m? (The unstretched position is at $x_0 = 0$.)

(a) 0.45 J   (b) 0.80 J   (c) 1.3 J   (d) 0.050 J   (e) 0.90 J

4.   A force of 200 N, directed at 20° above the horizontal, is applied to move a 50-kg cart (initially at rest) 10 m across a level surface. What is the speed of the cart at the end of the 10-m distance?

(a) 5.2 m/s   (b) 8.6 m/s   (c) 8.9 m/s   (d) 6.8×10^2 m/s   (e) 2.0×10^3 m/s

5.   A roller coaster makes a run down a track from a vertical distance of 25 m.   If there is negligible friction, and the coaster starts from rest, what is its speed at the bottom of the track?

(a) 5.0 m/s   (b) 16 m/s   (c) 22 m/s   (d) 2.5×10^2 m/s   (e) 4.9×10^2 m/s

6.   A 10-N force is needed to move an object with a constant velocity of 5.0 m/s. What power must be delivered to the object by the force?

(a) 0.50 W   (b) 1.0 W   (c) 2.0 W   (d) 50 W   (e) 100 W

7.   If it takes 50 m to stop a car initially moving at 15 m/s, what distance is required to stop a car moving at 30 m/s? (Assume the same braking force.)

(a) 25 m   (b) 50 m   (c) 100 m   (d) 150 m   (e) 200 m

8.   What is the minimum speed of the ball at the bottom of its swing (point B) in order for it to reach point A, which is 0.20 m above the bottom of the swing?

(a) 0.40 m/s   (b) 1.4 m/s   (c) 2.0 m/s   (d) 3.1 m/s   (e) 3.9 m/s

9.　A force of 10 N is applied horizontally to a 2.0-kg object on a level surface. The coefficient of kinetic friction between the object and the surface is 0.20. If the object is moved a distance of 10 m, what is the change in its kinetic energy?

(a) 100 J　　(b) 61 J　　(c) 46 J　　(d) 39 J　　(e) 20 J

10.　A 1500-kg car is moving with a speed of 25 m/s. How much work is required to stop the car?

(a) 1.5×10^3 J　　(b) 1.9×10^4 J　　(c) 3.8×10^4 J　　(d) 4.7×10^5 J　　(e) 9.4×10^5 J

11.　A 30-kg child slides down a playground slide from a height of 1.5 m above the bottom of the slide. If the child's speed at the bottom is 3.1 m/s, what is the work done by the nonconservative forces?

(a) 1.4×10^2 J　　(b) 3.0×10^2 J　　(c) 4.4×10^2 J　　(d) 5.9×10^2 J

12.　Water is lifted out of a 15-m-deep well by an electric motor rated at 1.5 hp. Assuming a 75% efficiency, what is the mass of water that can be lifted in one hour?

(a) 5.7 kg　　(b) 1.4×10^4 kg　　(c) 2.1×10^4 kg　　(d) 2.7×10^4 kg　　(e) 2.0×10^5 kg

Answers to Practice Quiz:

1. d 2. c 3. a 4. b 5. c 6. d 7. e 8. c 9. b 10. d 11. b 12. c

CHAPTER 6

Linear Momentum and Collisions

I. Chapter Objectives

Upon completion of this chapter, you should be able to:

1. compute linear momentum and the components of momentum.

2. relate impulse and momentum, and kinetic energy and momentum.

3. explain the condition for the conservation of linear momentum and apply it to physical situations.

4. describe the conditions on kinetic energy and momentum in elastic and inelastic collisions.

5. explain the concept of the center of mass and compute its location for simple systems, and describe how the center of mass and center of gravity are related.

*6. apply the conservation of momentum in the explanation of jet propulsion and the operation of rockets.

II. Chapter Summary and Discussion

1. Linear Momentum (Section 6.1)

The **linear momentum** of an object is defined as the product of its mass and velocity, $\mathbf{p} = m\mathbf{v}$. Because velocity is a vector, so is momentum. The SI units of momentum are kg·m/s.

Note: Momentum depends on *both* the mass and velocity, not just either mass or velocity.

The **total linear momentum** of a system is the vector sum of the momenta of the individual particles:

$$\mathbf{P} = \mathbf{p}_1 + \mathbf{p}_2 + \mathbf{p}_3 + \ldots = \sum_i \mathbf{p}_i$$

Note: An uppercase **P** is used for total momentum of the individual particles, and a lowercase **p** is used for the momentum of an individual particle.

Example 6.1   Which has more linear momentum:

   (a) a 1500-kg car moving at 25.0 m/s or

   (b) a 40 000-kg truck moving at 1.00 m/s?

Solution: Given: mass, m, and velocity, v.

Find: magnitude of momentum, p.

(a) $p = mv = (1500 \text{ kg})(25.0 \text{ m/s}) = 3.75 \times 10^4 \text{ kg·m/s}$.

(b) $p = (40\,000 \text{ kg})(1.00 \text{ m/s}) = 4.00 \times 10^4 \text{ kg·m/s}$.

The much slower truck has more momentum than the faster car because the truck has much greater mass.

Example 6.2   Two identical 1500-kg cars are moving perpendicular to each other. One is moving with a speed of 25.0 m/s due north, and the other is moving at 15.0 m/s due east. What is the total linear momentum of the system?

Solution: Given: $m_1 = m_2 = 1500 \text{ kg}$, $v_1 = 25.0 \text{ m/s}$, $v_2 = 15.0 \text{ m/s}$.

Find: **P**.

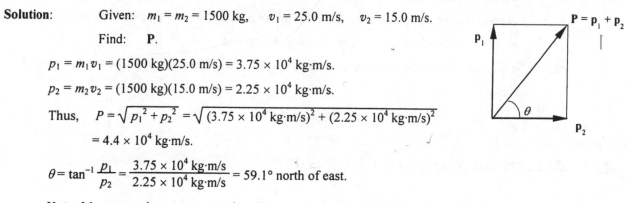

$p_1 = m_1 v_1 = (1500 \text{ kg})(25.0 \text{ m/s}) = 3.75 \times 10^4 \text{ kg·m/s}$.

$p_2 = m_2 v_2 = (1500 \text{ kg})(15.0 \text{ m/s}) = 2.25 \times 10^4 \text{ kg·m/s}$.

Thus, $P = \sqrt{p_1^2 + p_2^2} = \sqrt{(3.75 \times 10^4 \text{ kg·m/s})^2 + (2.25 \times 10^4 \text{ kg·m/s})^2}$

$= 4.4 \times 10^4 \text{ kg·m/s}$.

$\theta = \tan^{-1} \dfrac{p_1}{p_2} = \dfrac{3.75 \times 10^4 \text{ kg·m/s}}{2.25 \times 10^4 \text{ kg·m/s}} = 59.1°$ north of east.

Note: Momentum is a vector quantity. You must use vector addition when adding momenta.

Newton's second law can also be expressed in terms of momentum: $\mathbf{F}_{net} = \dfrac{\Delta \mathbf{p}}{\Delta t}$. It is equivalent to $\mathbf{F}_{net} = m\mathbf{a}$ if mass is a constant. (Actually, Newton used the momentum form of his second law when he first started formatting the law.) For system in which mass is not a constant, such as rocket propulsion, $\mathbf{F}_{net} = \dfrac{\Delta \mathbf{p}}{\Delta t}$ should be used. The impulse-momentum theorem discussed later is a variation of this form of Newton's second law.

2.   Impulse (Section 6.2)

From Newton's second law, $\mathbf{F}_{net} = \dfrac{\Delta \mathbf{p}}{\Delta t}$, we can derive the **impulse-momentum theorem**. This theorem states that *impulse is equal to the change in momentum*, or $\overline{\mathbf{F}} \Delta t = \Delta \mathbf{p} = \mathbf{p} - \mathbf{p}_o$, where $\overline{\mathbf{F}} \Delta t$ is called impulse ($\overline{\mathbf{F}}$ is the average force, and Δt is the time interval the force is in action).

Impulse-momentum is very useful in explaining some everyday phenomena. For example, why do tennis players follow through? Why do football players wear pads? Why can some not-so-strong martial artists break objects like bricks with their bare fists? Try to answer some of these questions, and the answers may surprise you.

Note: Again, momentum is a vector quantity and so must be treated as a vector. When opposite velocities are involved, you must choose one direction as positive. The direction opposite the positive direction will then be negative.

Example 6.3   A 0.10-kg ball is dropped onto a tabletop. The speed of the ball just before hitting the tabletop and just after hitting the tabletop is 5.0 m/s and 4.0 m/s, respectively. If the collision between the ball and the tabletop lasts 0.15 s, what is the average force exerted on the ball by the tabletop?

Solution: Given: $m = 0.10$ kg, $v_o = -5.0$ m/s (downward), $v = +4.0$ m/s (upward), $\Delta t = 0.15$ s.

Find: $\overline{F}$ (average force).

The velocity of the ball before the collision is downward, and the velocity of the ball after the collision is upward. Because these two velocities are opposite, we have to assign signs (+ or −) to them to find the change in velocity, Δv, properly. Conventionally, we choose the upward direction as positive, so the downward direction is negative. Thus, the initial velocity is negative, and the final velocity is positive. From the impulse-momentum theorem, $\overline{F} \Delta t = \Delta p = p - p_o$,

we have $\overline{F} = \dfrac{p - p_o}{\Delta t} = \dfrac{mv - mv_o}{\Delta t} = \dfrac{(0.10 \text{ kg})(4.0 \text{ m/s}) - (0.10 \text{ kg})(-5.0 \text{ m/s})}{0.15 \text{ s}} = +6.0$ N.

The positive sign indicates that the force on the ball by the tabletop is upward, which makes sense.

---

3.   The Conservation of Linear Momentum (Section 6.3)

The total linear momentum of a system is conserved if the net external force on the system is zero.

$$P = P_o, \quad \text{or} \quad p_1 + p_2 + \ldots = p_{1o} + p_{2o} + \ldots.$$

Note: Momentum is a vector quantity. You must use vector addition to determine the total momentum when applying the conservation of linear momentum.

When applied to a "collision" involving two objects, a more convenient form of the conservation of momentum can be written as $m_1 v_1 + m_2 v_2 = m_1 v_{1o} + m_2 v_{2o}$, where the m's are the masses of the two objects, the v_o's are the initial velocities, and the v's are the final velocities.

Note: The terms *initial* and *final* are always relative, and here they are relative to the "collision" process. A collision is generally defined in physics as a process in which forces are exchanged.

Example 6.4   A 50-kg pitching machine (excluding the baseball) is placed on a frozen pond. The machine fires a 0.40-kg baseball with a speed of 35 m/s in the horizontal direction. What is the recoil velocity of the pitching machine? (Assume negligible friction.)

Solution: Given: $m_1 = 50$ kg (machine) $m_2 = 0.40$ kg (ball)

   $v_{1o} = 0$ $v_{2o} = 0$

   $v_2 = 35$ m/s

   Find: v_1.

Here the "collision" process is the firing of the baseball. Before the baseball is fired, neither the machine nor the baseball is moving, so both have zero initial velocity and momentum (the total initial momentum P_o is zero). After the ball is fired, the ball moves in one direction, and the machine must recoil in the opposite direction so that the total momentum P is zero.

From momentum conservation, $\mathbf{P} = \mathbf{P}_o$,   or $\mathbf{p}_1 + \mathbf{p}_2 = \mathbf{p}_{1o} + \mathbf{p}_{2o}$,

we have $m_1 v_1 + m_2 v_2 = m_1 v_{1o} + m_2 v_{2o} = 0$.

Thus, $v_1 = -\dfrac{m_2 v_2}{m_1} = -\dfrac{(0.40 \text{ kg})(35 \text{ m/s})}{50 \text{ kg}} = -0.28$ m/s.

The negative sign here indicates the machine is moving in exactly the opposite direction of the ball.

Example 6.5   A 10-g bullet moving at 300 m/s is fired into a 1.0-kg block. The bullet emerges (does not stay embedded in the block) with half of its original speed. What is the velocity of the block right after the collision?

Solution: Given $m_1 = 0.010$ kg (bullet) $m_2 = 1.0$ kg (block)

   $v_{1o} = 300$ m/s $v_{2o} = 0$

   $v_1 = 150$ m/s

   Find: v_2.

Right before the bullet hits the block, the bullet is moving at 300 m/s and the block is at rest. Right after the bullet hits the block, the bullet emerges at (300 m/s)/2 = 150 m/s, and the block should be moving in the same direction as the bullet. (Why?)

From momentum conservation, $\mathbf{P} = \mathbf{P}_o$,   or $\mathbf{p}_1 + \mathbf{p}_2 = \mathbf{p}_{1o} + \mathbf{p}_{2o}$,

we have $m_1 v_1 + m_2 v_2 = m_1 v_{1o} + m_2 v_{2o} = m_1 v_{1o} + 0 = m_1 v_{1o}$.

Thus, $v_2 = \dfrac{m_1 v_{1o} - m_1 v_1}{m_2} = \dfrac{(0.010 \text{ kg})(300 \text{ m/s} - 150 \text{ m/s})}{1.0 \text{ kg}} = +1.5$ m/s.

The result is positive because the block is moving in the same direction as the bullet.

---

4. Elastic and Inelastic Collision (Section 6.4)

Linear momentum is always conserved in a collision as long as the net external force is zero on the system, which is approximately true at least during the small time interval Δt of the collision; however, in an **elastic collision**, kinetic energy is also conserved, whereas in an **inelastic collision**, kinetic energy is not conserved. (**Note:** When kinetic energy is not conserved, as is the usual case, this does not mean the *total energy* is not conserved. Some of the kinetic energy is converted to heat, sound, or other forms. during a collision. Total energy is always conserved, as we shall see!). If the objects in a system stick together after collision, the collision is called **completely inelastic**. In an inelastic collision, the kinetic energy of the system before the collision is always greater than the kinetic energy of the system after the collision. Why?

Example 6.6   While standing on skates on a frozen pond, a student of mass 70.0 kg catches a 2.00-kg ball traveling horizontally at 15.0 m/s toward him.

(a) What is the speed of the student and the ball immediately after he catches it?

(b) How much kinetic energy is lost in the process?

Solution: Given: $m_1 = 70.0$ kg $m_2 = 2.00$ kg

$\qquad\qquad\qquad v_{1o} = 0$ $v_{2o} = 15.0$ m/s

$\qquad\quad$ Find: v_1 v_2.

Because the student catches the ball, they must have the same final velocity, $v_1 = v_2 = v$. Here the "collision" is the catching action.

(a) From momentum conservation, $\mathbf{P} = \mathbf{P}_o$,   or $\mathbf{p}_1 + \mathbf{p}_2 = \mathbf{p}_{1o} + \mathbf{p}_{2o}$,

we have $m_1 v_1 + m_2 v_2 = m_1 v + m_2 v = (m_1 + m_2)v = m_1 v_{1o} + m_2 v_{2o}$.

Thus, $v = \dfrac{m_1 v_{1o} + m_2 v_{2o}}{m_1 + m_2} = \dfrac{(70.0 \text{ kg})(0) + (2.00 \text{ kg})(15.0 \text{ m/s})}{70.0 \text{ kg} + 2.00 \text{ kg}} = 0.417$ m/s.

(b) Initial kinetic energy: $K_o = \frac{1}{2} m_1 v_{1o}^2 + \frac{1}{2} m_2 v_{2o}^2 = \frac{1}{2}(70.0 \text{ kg})(0)^2 + \frac{1}{2}(2.00 \text{ kg})(15.0 \text{ m/s})^2 = 225$ J.

Final kinetic energy: $K = \frac{1}{2} m_1 v_1^2 + \frac{1}{2} m_2 v_2^2 = \frac{1}{2}[(70.0 \text{ kg}) + (2.00 \text{ kg})](0.417 \text{ m/s})^2 = 6.26$ J.

Thus, the kinetic energy lost in the collision is $|\Delta K| = K_o - K = 225 \text{ J} - 6.26 \text{ J} = 219$ J.

The percentage of kinetic energy loss is $\dfrac{K - K_o}{K_o} = \dfrac{-219 \text{ J}}{225 \text{ J}} = -0.97 = -97\%$.

Example 6.7   A rubber ball with a speed of 5.0 m/s collides head on elastically with an identical ball at rest. Find the velocity of each object after the collision.

Solution:

Given: $m_1 = m$ $m_2 = m$ (identical ball)

$v_{1_o} = 5.0$ m/s $v_{2_o} = 0$

Find: v_1 v_2.

This is an elastic collision, and we use Eqs. (6.15) and (6.16).

$$v_1 = \left(\frac{m_1 - m_2}{m_1 + m_2}\right) v_{1_o} = \frac{m - m}{m + m} (5.0 \text{ m/s}) = 0; \quad v_2 = \left(\frac{2m_1}{m_1 + m_2}\right) v_{1_o} = \frac{2m}{m + m} (5.0 \text{ m/s}) = 5.0 \text{ m/s}.$$

The two balls exchange velocities. This is always the case if $m_1 = m_2$ in such collisions.

---

5.   Center of Mass (Section 6.5)

The **center of mass** of a system is the point at which all the mass of the system may be considered to be concentrated. If the acceleration due to gravity, g, is a constant, then the **center of gravity**, or the point at which all the weight of the system may be considered to be concentrated, is at the center of mass. For a system of particles, the

coordinates of the center of mass are calculated from $X_{CM} = \dfrac{\sum_i m_i x_i}{M}$ and $Y_{CM} = \dfrac{\sum_i m_i y_i}{M}$, where x_i and y_i are the

coordinates of the particle m_i, and $M = \sum_i m_i$ is the total mass of the system.

The motion of the center of mass also obeys Newton's second law: $\mathbf{F}_{net\ external} = M\mathbf{A}_{CM}$, where $\mathbf{F}_{net\ external}$ is the net external force, M is the total mass of the system, and $\mathbf{A}_{CM}$ is the acceleration of the center of mass.

Example 6.8   Find the location of the center of mass of the following three-mass system.

Mass	Location
$m_1 = 1.0$ kg	$(0, 0)$
$m_2 = 2.0$ kg	$(1.0$ m, 1.0 m$)$
$m_3 = 3.0$ kg	$(2.0$ m, -2.0 m$)$

Solution:

$$X_{CM} = \frac{\sum_i m_i x_i}{M} = \frac{(1.0 \text{ kg})(0) + (2.0 \text{ kg})(1.0 \text{ m}) + (3.0 \text{ kg})(2.0 \text{ m})}{1.0 \text{ kg} + 2.0 \text{ kg} + 3.0 \text{ kg}} = 1.3 \text{ m}.$$

$$Y_{CM} = \frac{\sum_i m_i y_i}{M} = \frac{(1.0 \text{ kg})(0) + (2.0 \text{ kg})(1.0 \text{ m}) + (3.0 \text{ kg})(-2.0 \text{ m})}{1.0 \text{ kg} + 2.0 \text{ kg} + 3.0 \text{ kg}} = -0.67 \text{ m}.$$

Thus, the location of the center of mass is at $(X_{CM}, Y_{CM}) = (1.3 \text{ m}, -0.67 \text{ m})$.

III. Mathematical Summary

Linear Momentum	$\mathbf{p} = m\mathbf{v}$ (6.1)	Defines linear momentum.
Total Linear Momentum	$\mathbf{P} = \mathbf{p}_1 + \mathbf{p}_2 + \mathbf{p}_3 + \ldots$ $= \sum_i \mathbf{p}_i$ (6.2)	Computes total linear momentum of a system.
Newton's Second Law in terms of Momentum	$\mathbf{F}_{net} = \dfrac{\Delta \mathbf{p}}{\Delta t}$ (6.3)	Rewrites Newton's second law in terms of momentum.
Impulse-momentum theorem	Impulse = $\overline{\mathbf{F}} \, \Delta t = \Delta \mathbf{p} = m\mathbf{v} - m\mathbf{v}_0$ (6.5)	States that the impulse is equal to the change in momentum.
Conditions for an Elastic Collision	$\mathbf{P}_f = \mathbf{P}_i, \quad K_f = K_i$ (6.8)	Defines the conditions for an elastic collision.
Conditions for an Inelastic Collision	$\mathbf{P}_f = \mathbf{P}_i, \quad K_f < K_i$ (6.9)	Defines the conditions for an inelastic collision.
Final Velocities in Head-On Elastic Collision ($v_{2_0} = 0$)	$v_1 = \left(\dfrac{m_1 - m_2}{m_1 + m_2}\right) v_{1o}$ (6.15) $v_2 = \left(\dfrac{2m_1}{m_1 + m_2}\right) v_{1o}$ (6.16)	Expresses the final velocities in head-on elastic collisions.
Coordinate of center of Mass (using sign for directions)	$X_{CM} = \dfrac{\sum_i m_i x_i}{M}$ (6.20)	Calculates the coordinate of the center of mass of a system (using signs for directions).

IV. Solutions of Selected Exercises and Paired Exercises

8.   (a) Momentum is $p = mv = (7.1 \text{ kg})(12 \text{ m/s}) = \boxed{85 \text{ kg·m/s}}$.

      (b) 90 km/h = 25 m/s. $p = (1200 \text{ kg})(25 \text{ m/s}) = \boxed{3.0 \times 10^4 \text{ kg·m/s}}$.

12.   Because the ball moves in the opposite direction, we chose the initial direction of velocity as the positive velocity direction. $v = -34.7$ m/s   and $v_0 = 4.50$ m/s.

      $\Delta p = mv - mv_0 = (0.150 \text{ kg})(-34.7 \text{ m/s}) - (0.150 \text{ kg})(4.50 \text{ m/s}) = \boxed{-5.88 \text{ kg·m/s}}$.

      The negative sign means that the change in momentum is in the direction opposite the initial velocity.

17. $P = p_1 + p_2 = \pm 350$ kg·m/s. It can be either positive or negative because the exercise does not specify the direction of the momentum.

± 350 kg·m/s $= (70$ kg$)(2.0$ m/s$) + (60$ kg$)v_2$,   so $v_2 = +3.5$ m/s or -8.2 m/s.

The velocity of the light runner is $\boxed{3.5 \text{ m/s in the same direction or 8.2 m/s in the opposite direction}}$.

20. From Newton's second law in terms of momentum, we have

$$\overline{F} = \frac{\Delta p}{\Delta t} = \frac{mv - mv_0}{\Delta t} = \frac{(10 \text{ kg})(4.0 \text{ m/s} - 0)}{2.5 \text{ s}} = \boxed{16 \text{ N}}.$$

30. Apply the impulse-momentum theorem to the horizontal motion.

$$\overline{F}\Delta t = mv - mv_0 = mv, \quad \text{so} \quad v = \frac{\overline{F}\Delta t}{m} = \frac{3.0 \text{ N·s}}{0.20 \text{ kg}} = \boxed{15 \text{ m/s}}.$$

35. (a) $\boxed{\text{Hitting it back}}$ requires a greater force. Force is proportional to the change in momentum. When a ball changes its direction, the change in momentum is greater. If $\mathbf{p} = \mathbf{p}_1 - \mathbf{p}_2$ and $\mathbf{p}_1$ and $\mathbf{p}_2$ are opposite (hitting it back), then $p = p_1 - (-p_2) = p_1 + p_2$. Had you caught the ball, then $p_2 = 0$, so $p = p_1$.

(b) The final velocity is opposite the initial velocity ("hitting it back"), so the final velocity is negative. From the impulse-momentum theorem, we have

$$\overline{F} = \frac{\Delta p}{\Delta t} = \frac{mv - mv_0}{\Delta t} = \frac{(0.45 \text{ kg})(-7.0 \text{ m/s} - 4.0 \text{ m/s})}{0.040 \text{ s}} = \boxed{-1.2 \times 10^2 \text{ N}}.$$

The negative sign means that the average force is in the direction opposite the initial velocity.

41. 40 km/h $= 11.1$ m/s,   2400 lb $= 10\,680$ N.

The force on the infant is opposite the velocity, so it is taken as a negative value..

From the impulse momentum theorem, $F\Delta t = mv - mv_0$, we have

$$\Delta t = \frac{mv - mv_0}{F} = \frac{(55 \text{ kg})(0 - 11.1 \text{ m/s})}{-10\,680 \text{ N}} = \boxed{0.057 \text{ s}}.$$

48. According to the conservation of momentum, the astronaut moves in the opposite direction.

$m_1 = 0.50$ kg, $m_2 = 60$ kg, $v_{1o} = 0$, $v_{2o} = 0$, $v_1 = 10$ m/s, $v_2 = ?$

From the conservation of momentum, $\mathbf{P}_o = \mathbf{P}$, we have $m_1 v_{1o} + m_2 v_{2o} = m_1 v_1 + m_2 v_2$.

$$v_2 = \frac{m_1 v_{1o} + m_2 v_{2o} - m_1 v_1}{m_2} = \frac{0 + 0 - (0.50 \text{ kg})(10 \text{ m/s})}{60 \text{ kg}} = \boxed{0.083 \text{ m/s in the opposite direction}}.$$

52. (a) According to momentum conservation, the total momentum of the three-fragment system must be zero. Therefore, the third fragment must fly off toward a general direction of $\boxed{\text{north of east}}$.

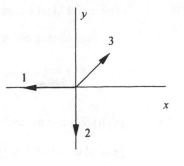

(b) Apply momentum conservation $\mathbf{P}_o = \mathbf{P}$

along the x-axis:

$(2.0 \text{ kg})(0) = (0.50 \text{ kg})(-2.8 \text{ m/s}) + (1.3 \text{ kg})(0) + (1.2 \text{ kg})v_x$,

so $v_x = 1.17 \text{ m/s}$;

along the y-axis:

$(3.0 \text{ kg})(0) = (0.50 \text{ kg})(0) + (1.3 \text{ kg})(-1.5 \text{ m/s}) + (1.2 \text{ kg})v_y$,

so $v_y = 1.63 \text{ m/s}$.

Therefore, $v = \sqrt{(1.17 \text{ m/s})^2 + (1.63 \text{ m/s})^2} = \boxed{2.0 \text{ m/s}}$,

$$\theta = \tan^{-1}\left(\frac{1.63}{1.17}\right) = \boxed{54° \text{ north of east}}.$$

55. $m_1 = 1200 \text{ kg}$, $m_2 = 1500 \text{ kg}$, $v_{1o} = 25 \text{ m/s}$, $v_1 = v_2 = v$? (coupling)

From momentum conservation, $\mathbf{P}_o = \mathbf{P}$,

we have $m_1 v_{1o} + m_2 v_{2o} = (m_1 + m_2)v$, so $v = \dfrac{m_1 v_{1o} + m_2 v_{2o}}{m_1 + m_2}$.

(a) $v = \dfrac{(1200 \text{ kg})(25 \text{ m/s}) + (0)}{1200 \text{ kg} + 1500 \text{ kg}} = \boxed{11 \text{ m/s to the right}}$.

(b) $v = \dfrac{(1200 \text{ kg})(25 \text{ m/s}) + (1500 \text{ kg})(20 \text{ m/s})}{1200 \text{ kg} + 1500 \text{ kg}} = \boxed{22 \text{ m/s to the right}}$.

(c) $v = \dfrac{(1200 \text{ kg})(25 \text{ m/s}) + (1500 \text{ kg})(-20 \text{ m/s})}{1200 \text{ kg} + 1500 \text{ kg}} = 0$ or $\boxed{\text{at rest}}$.

66. This is an elastic collision, and we use Eqs. (6.15) and (6.16).

$v_1 = \dfrac{m_1 - m_2}{m_1 + m_2} v_{1o} = \dfrac{4.0 \text{ kg} - 2.0 \text{ kg}}{4.0 \text{ kg} + 2.0 \text{ kg}} (4.0 \text{ m/s}) = \boxed{+1.3 \text{ m/s}}$.

$v_2 = \dfrac{2m_1}{m_1 + m_2} v_{1o} = \dfrac{2(4.0 \text{ kg})}{4.0 \text{ kg} + 2.0 \text{ kg}} (4.0 \text{ m/s}) = \boxed{+5.3 \text{ m/s}}$.

70. We first find the velocity of the 6.0-kg ball right after collision from momentum conservation, $\mathbf{P}_o = \mathbf{P}$.

$m_1 = 2.0 \text{ kg}$, $m_2 = 6.0 \text{ kg}$, $v_{1o} = 12 \text{ m/s}$, $v_{2o} = -4.0 \text{ m/s}$ ("toward each other"),

$v_1 = -8.0 \text{ m/s}$ ("recoil").

$(2.0 \text{ kg})(12 \text{ m/s}) + (6.0 \text{ kg})(-4.0 \text{ m/s}) = (2.0 \text{ kg})(-8.0 \text{ m/s}) + (6.0 \text{ kg})v_2$, so $v_2 = 2.67 \text{ m/s}$.

The initial kinetic energy is $\qquad$ $K_o = \frac{1}{2}(2.0\ \text{kg})(12\ \text{m/s})^2 + \frac{1}{2}(6.0\ \text{kg})(4.0\ \text{m/s})^2 = 192\ \text{J}$;

The final kinetic energy is $\qquad$ $K = \frac{1}{2}(2.0\ \text{kg})(8.0\ \text{m/s})^2 + \frac{1}{2}(6.0\ \text{kg})(2.67\ \text{m/s})^2 = 84.5\ \text{J}$.

Thus, the kinetic energy lost is $K_o - K = \boxed{1.1 \times 10^2\ \text{J}}$.

73. (a) Right after the collision, the car and minivan will move toward a general direction $\boxed{\text{south of east}}$ according to momentum conservation.

The initial momentum of the minivan is to the south, and the initial momentum of the car is to the east, so the two-vehicle system has a total momentum to the southeast and that remains after the collision.

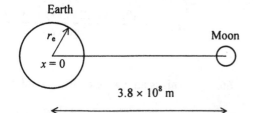

(b) 90.0 km/h = 25.0 m/s, $\quad$ 60.0 km/h = 16.67 m/s.

Apply momentum conservation, $\mathbf{P}_o = \mathbf{P}$,

along the x-axis:

$(1500\ \text{kg})(25.0\ \text{m/s}) + (3000\ \text{kg})(0) = (1500\ \text{kg} + 3000\ \text{kg})v'_x$, $\quad$ so $\quad$ $v'_x = 8.33\ \text{m/s}$.

along the y-axis:

$(1500\ \text{kg})(0) - (3000\ \text{kg})(16.67\ \text{m/s}) = (1500\ \text{kg} + 3000\ \text{kg})v'_y$, $\quad$ so $\quad$ $v'_y = -11.1\ \text{m/s}$.

Therefore, $\qquad$ $v' = \sqrt{(8.33\ \text{m/s})^2 + (-11.1\ \text{m/s})^2} = \boxed{13.9\ \text{m/s}}$,

and $\qquad$ $\theta = \tan^{-1}\dfrac{-11.1\ \text{m/s}}{8.33\ \text{m/s}} = \boxed{53.1°\ \text{south of east}}$.

89. (a) $X_{CM} = \dfrac{\Sigma_i\, m_i x_i}{M} = \dfrac{(6.0\times10^{24}\ \text{kg})(0) + (6.4\times10^{22}\ \text{kg})(3.8\times10^8\ \text{m})}{6.0\times10^{24}\ \text{kg} + 7.4\times10^{22}\ \text{kg}}$

$= \boxed{4.6 \times 10^6\ \text{m from the center of the Earth}}$.

(b) From the surface of the Earth, it is at

$4.6 \times 10^6\ \text{m} - r_e = 4.6 \times 10^6\ \text{m} - 7.37 \times 10^6\ \text{m} = -1.8 \times 10^6\ \text{m}$,

i.e., $\boxed{1.8 \times 10^6\ \text{m below the surface of the Earth}}$.

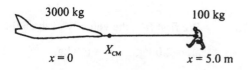

96. Due to the lack of external force, the CM is stationary and is at the point where they meet.

$X_{CM} = \dfrac{\Sigma_i\, m_i x_i}{M} = \dfrac{(3000\ \text{kg})(0) + (100\ \text{kg})(5.0\ \text{m})}{3000\ \text{kg} + 100\ \text{kg}}$

$= \boxed{0.16\ \text{m from capsule's original position}}$.

105.   (a) Apply momentum conservation $\mathbf{P}_o = \mathbf{P}$,

along the x-axis:

$$\frac{7500\ N}{g}(60\ km/h) + \frac{15\,000\ N}{g}(0) = \frac{7500\ N}{g}v_x + \frac{15\,000\ N}{g}v_x,$$

so $v_x = 20$ km/h.

along the y-axis:

$$\frac{7500\ N}{g}(0) + \frac{15\,000\ N}{g}(45\ km/h) = \frac{7500\ N}{g}v_y + \frac{15\,000\ N}{g}v_y,$$

so $v_y = 30$ km/h.

Therefore, $v = \sqrt{(20\ km/h)^2 + (30\ km/h)^2} = \boxed{36\ km/h}$, $\theta = \tan^{-1}\left(\frac{30}{20}\right) = \boxed{56°\ \text{north of east}}$.

(b) The percentage of kinetic energy lost is

$$\frac{|\Delta K|}{K_o} = \frac{K_o - K}{K_o} = 1 - \frac{K}{K_o} = 1 - \frac{\frac{1}{2}(7500 + 15\,000)(36)^2}{\frac{1}{2}(7500)(60)^2 + \frac{1}{2}(15\,000)(45)^2} = 1 - 0.51 = \boxed{49\%}.$$

V.   Practice Quiz

1.   The SI unit of impulse is which one of the following?

(a) N·m   (b) N/s   (c) N·s   (d) N/m   (e) kg·m/s^2

2.   A force of 10 N acts on a 5.0-kg object, initially at rest, for 2.5 s. What is the final speed of the object?

(a) 1.0 m/s   (b) 2.0 m/s   (c) 3.0 m/s   (d) 4.0 m/s   (e) 5.0 m/s

3.   A 70-kg astronaut is space walking outside the space capsule and is stationary when the tether line breaks.
As a means of returning to the capsule he throws his 2.0-kg space wrench at a speed of 14 m/s away from
the capsule. At what speed does the astronaut move toward the capsule?

(a) 0.40 m/s   (b) 1.5 m/s   (c) 3.5 m/s   (d) 5.0 m/s   (e) 7.0 m/s

4.   A 1500-kg car, is allowed to coast along a level track at a speed of 8.0 m/s. It collides and couples with a
2000-kg truck, initially at rest and with brakes released. What is the speed of the two vehicles after they
collide?

(a) 0.75 m/s   (b) 3.4 m/s   (c) 4.6 m/s   (d) 6.0 m/s   (e) 11 m/s

5.   A 0.060-kg tennis ball, initially moving at a speed of 12 m/s, is struck, which causes it to rebound in the
opposite direction at a speed of 18 m/s. What is the change in momentum of the ball?

(a) 0.18 kg·m/s   (b) 0.36 kg·m/s   (c) 0.72 kg·m/s   (d) 1.1 kg·m/s   (e) 1.8 kg·m/s.

6. The center of mass of a two-particle system is at the origin. One particle is located at (3.0 m, 0 m) and has a mass of 2.0 kg. What is the location of the second mass of 4.0 kg?

   (a) (−3.0 m, 0 m)   (b) (−2.0 m, 0 m)   (c) (−1.5 m, 0 m)   (d) (−0.75 m, 0 m)   (e) (−0.50 m, 0 m)

7. In an elastic collision, if the momentum of the system is conserved, then which of the following statements is true about kinetic energy?

   (a) Kinetic energy is also conserved.   (b) Kinetic energy is gained.

   (c) Kinetic energy is lost.   (d) Kinetic energy is halved.

   (e) none of the preceding

8. A 0.10-kg object with a velocity of 0.20 m/s in the +x-direction makes a head-on elastic collision with a 0.15-kg object initially at rest. What is the velocity of the 0.10-kg object after collision?

   (a) −0.16 m/s   (b) +0.16 m/s   (c) 0   (d) −0.040 m/s   (e) +0.040 m/s

9. If the momentum of an object is halved, what is the ratio of the new kinetic energy to the initial kinetic energy?

   (a) 2   (b) 4   (c) 0   (d) 1/2   (e) 1/4

10. Standing on a frozen pond, a student throws a baseball horizontalLY in one direction. What happens to the center of mass of the student-baseball system?

    (a) it goes up.   (b) it is stationary.   (c) it follows the path of the rocket.

    (d) it follows the path of the fuel.   (e) not enough information is given.

11. A 1500-kg truck moving with a speed of 25 m/s runs into the rear of a 1200-kg stopped car. If the collision is perfectly inelastic, what is the kinetic energy lost in the collision?

    (a) 1.2×10^5 J   (b) 2.1×10^5 J   (c) 2.4×10^5 J   (d) 3.8×10^5 J   (e) 4.7×10^5 J

12. A 0.35-kg mud ball is dropped from a height of 2.5 m above a floor. When it hits the floor, the mud ball comes to rest in 0.30 s. What is the magnitude of the average force on the mud ball by the floor?

    (a) 1.7 N   (b) 2.9 N   (c) 5.8 N   (d) 8.2 N   (e) 57 N

Answers to Practice Quiz:

1. c 2. e 3. a 4. b 5. e 6. c 7. a 8. d 9. e 10. b 11. b 12. d

CHAPTER 7

Solids and Fluids

I. Chapter Objectives

Upon completion of this chapter, you should be able to:

1. distinguish between stress and strain, and use elastic moduli to compute dimensional changes.

2. explain the pressure–depth relationship, state Pascal's principle, and describe how it is used in practical applications.

3. relate the buoyant force and Archimedes' principle and tell whether an object will float in a fluid, on the basis of relative densities.

4. identify the simplifications used in describing ideal fluid flow, and use the continuity equation and Bernoulli's equation to explain common effects of ideal fluid flow.

*5. describe the source of surface tension and its effect, and discuss fluid viscosity.

II. Chapter Summary and Discussion

1. Solids and Elastic Moduli (Section 7.1)

All materials are elastic to some degree and can be deformed. **Stress** is the quantity that describes the force causing the deformation, and **strain** is a relative measure of how much deformation a given stress produces. Quantitatively, stress is the applied force per unit cross-sectional area, and strain is the ratio of the change in dimensions to the original dimensions.

$$\text{Stress} = \frac{F}{A}, \text{ tensile strain (in length)} = \frac{\Delta L}{L_0}, \text{ shear strain (in area)} = \frac{x}{h}, \text{ volume strain} = \frac{\Delta V}{V_0}.$$

In general, stress is proportional to strain up to the elastic limit. The constant of proportionality, which depends on the nature of the material, is called the **elastic modulus** and is defined as the ratio of stress to strain,

$$\text{elastic modulus} = \frac{\text{stress}}{\text{strain}}.$$

There are three types of elastic moduli, the Young's modulus Y, the shear modulus S, and the bulk modulus B. $Y = \frac{F/A}{\Delta L/L_0}$, $S = \frac{F/A}{x/h} \approx \frac{F/A}{\phi}$, $B = \frac{F/A}{-\Delta V/V_0} = -\frac{\Delta p}{\Delta V/V_0}$. The SI units of moduli are N/m^2 or pascal (Pa). The compressibility is the inverse of the bulk modulus, $k = \frac{1}{B}$ (for gases).

Example 7.1   A steel wire 2.0 m in length and 2.0 mm in diameter supports a 10-kg object.

(a) What is the stress in the wire?

(b) What is the elongation of the wire?

Solution: Given: $F = w = mg = (10 \text{ kg})(9.80 \text{ m/s}^2) = 98 \text{ N}$, $L_0 = 2.0 \text{ m}$,

$r = d/2 = 1.0 \text{ mm} = 1.0 \times 10^{-3} \text{ m}$, $Y = 20 \times 10^{10} \text{ N/m}^2$ (from Table 9.1).

Find: (a) stress $= F/A$ (b) ΔL.

(a) Stress $= \dfrac{F}{A} = \dfrac{F}{\pi r^2} = \dfrac{98 \text{ N}}{\pi (1.0 \times 10^{-3} \text{ m})^2} = 3.1 \times 10^7 \text{ N/m}^2$.

(b) From the definition of Young's modulus, $Y = \dfrac{F/A}{\Delta L/L_0} = \dfrac{L_0(F/A)}{\Delta L}$,

we have $\Delta L = \dfrac{L_0(F/A)}{Y} = \dfrac{(2.0 \text{ m})(3.1 \times 10^7 \text{ N/m}^2)}{(20 \times 10^{10} \text{ N/m}^2)} = 3.1 \times 10^{-4} \text{ m} = 0.31 \text{ mm}$.

Example 7.2   A shear force of 2.0×10^3 N is applied to one face of an aluminum cube with sides of 15 cm. What is the resulting relative displacement?

Solution: Given: $F = 2.0 \times 10^3$ N, $h = 0.15$ m, $S = 2.5 \times 10^{10}$ N/m^2 (from Table 9.1).

Find: x.

The area of a side is $A = h^2$.

From $S = \dfrac{F/A}{x/h}$,

we have $x = \dfrac{F/A}{S/h} = \dfrac{Fh}{AS} = \dfrac{Fh}{h^2 S} = \dfrac{F}{hS} = \dfrac{2.0 \times 10^3 \text{ N}}{(0.15 \text{ m})(2.5 \times 10^{10} \text{ N/m}^2)} = 5.3 \times 10^{-7} \text{ m}$.

2.   Fluids: Pressure and Pascal's Principle (Section 7.2)

A **fluid** is a substance that flows and cannot support a shear. Both liquids and gases are fluids. **Pressure** is defined as the force per unit area, $P = \dfrac{F}{A}$, and has units of N/m^2 or pascal (Pa).

Absolute pressure on an object submerged at a depth h below the surface of a fluid is given by the **pressure-depth equation**, $p = p_0 + \rho g h$, where p_0 is the pressure on the fluid surface, and ρ is the density of the fluid. When this equation is applied to fluid on the surface of the Earth, $p_o = p_a = 1.01 \times 10^5$ Pa, where p_a is called the atmospheric pressure and is measured with a barometer. **Gauge pressure** (static pressure) is the difference between the absolute pressure and the atmospheric pressure, that is, $p_{gauge} = p - p_a = \rho g h$. When a pressure gauge is used to measure pressure, it measures the gauge pressure.

Pascal's principle states that any external pressure applied to an *enclosed* fluid is transmitted undiminished to every point in the fluid and to the walls of its container.

A hydraulic press and a hydraulic lift are good practical applications of this principle. In a press or lift, there are usually two pistons, one with a larger area than the other. If a small force, F_i, is applied to the smaller (input) piston of cross-sectional area A_i, the external pressure on the input piston is then $p_i = \dfrac{F_i}{A_i}$. According to Pascal's principle, this pressure will be transmitted to the larger (output) piston of cross-sectional area A_o, and $p_o = p_i$ or $\dfrac{F_o}{A_o} = \dfrac{F_i}{A_i}$. Since $A_o > A_i, F_o > F_i$.

Example 7.3   (a) What is the absolute pressure at a location 5.00 m below the surface of a freshwater lake?
(b) What is the gauge pressure there?

Solution: Given: $p_o = p_a = 1.01 \times 10^5$ Pa, $h = 5.00$ m, $\rho = 1.00 \times 10^3$ kg/m^3 (water from Table 9.2)
Find: (a) p (b) $p_{gauge} = p - p_o$ (gauge pressure).

(a) $p = p_o + \rho g h = 1.01 \times 10^5$ Pa $+ (1.00 \times 10^3$ kg/m$^3)(9.80$ m/s$^2)(5.00$ m$) = 1.50 \times 10^5$ Pa.

(b) $p_{gauge} = p - p_a = 1.50 \times 10^5$ Pa $- 1.01 \times 10^5$ Pa $= 4.9 \times 10^4$ Pa.

Example 7.4   In a hydraulic garage lift, the small piston has a radius of 5.0 cm, and the large piston has a radius of 15 cm. What force must be applied on the small piston in order to lift a car weighing 20 000 N on the large piston?

Solution: Given: $r_i = 0.050$ m, $r_o = 0.15$ m, $F_o = 20\,000$ N.
Find: F_i.

According to Pascal's principle, the external pressure exerted at the small piston is transmitted undiminished to the large piston. Therefore, $p_i = \dfrac{F_i}{A_i} = p_o = \dfrac{F_o}{A_o}$.

Thus, $F_i = \left(\dfrac{A_i}{A_o}\right) F_o = \left(\dfrac{\pi r_i^2}{\pi r_o^2}\right) F_o = \left(\dfrac{r_i}{r_o}\right)^2 F_o = \left(\dfrac{0.050}{0.15}\right)^2 (20\,000$ N$) \approx 2200$ N.

Note: What a wonderful device! The radius of the large piston is only three times the radius of the small piston, $(0.15 \text{ m})/(0.050 \text{ m}) = 3$; however, the force required on the small piston is only 1/9 of the force on the large piston, $\dfrac{2200 \text{ N}}{20\ 000 \text{ N}} = 1/9$. Why?

---

3. Buoyancy and Archimedes' Principle (Section 7.3)

An object that is either partially or completely submerged in a fluid will experience an upward buoyant force exerted by the fluid. **Archimedes' principle** states that the buoyant force is equal to the weight of the fluid displaced by the object, that is, if an object displaces 3.0 N of fluid, it will experience a 3.0 N buoyant force. Mathematically, the principle is expressed as $F_b = w_f = m_f g = (\rho_f V_f)g = \rho_f V_f g$, where ρ_f is the density of the fluid, V_f is the volume of fluid displaced (which is the same as the volume fraction of the object submerged *in* the fluid).

Archimedes' principle is very useful in determining the volume of an object and therefore its density and was what Archimedes allegedly used to determine that the crown of his king was not made of pure gold.

From Archimedes' principle, we can draw some simple conclusions about density and floating:

(1) An object will float in a fluid if the average density of the object is less than the density of the fluid.
(2) An object will sink in a fluid if the average density of the object is greater than the density of the fluid.
(3) An object will be in equilibrium at any submerged depth in a fluid if the average densities of the object and fluid are equal.

The **specific gravity** (*sp. gr.*) of a substance is the ratio of the density of the substance to the density of water, and so is a pure number (dimensionless). For example, aluminum has a density of 2700 kg/m^3, and water has a density of 1000 kg/m^3. Thus, the specific gravity (*sp. gr.*) of aluminum is simply (2700 kg/m^3)/(1000 kg/m^3) = 2.7.

Example 7.5 A boat approximating a rectangular box measures 5.0 m long, 1.0 wide and 0.50 m high. Is it safe to transport a 3000-kg machine part with this boat across a lake? (Neglect the mass of the boat itself.)

Solution: Given: $L = 5.0$ m, $W = 1.0$ m, $H = 0.50$ m, $\rho_{water} = 1.0 \times 10^3$ kg/m^3, $m = 3000$ kg.

Find: Will the boat float or sink?

The average density of the boat (with the machine part) is

$$\rho = \frac{m}{V} = \frac{3000 \text{ kg}}{(5.0 \text{ m})(1.0 \text{ m})(0.50 \text{ m})} = 1.2 \times 10^4 \text{ kg/m}^3 > \rho_{water} = 1.0 \times 10^3 \text{ kg/m}^3.$$

Because the average density of the boats is greater than that of water, the boat will sink, so it is not safe to transport the machine part with this boat.

Example 7.6   A bargain hunter buys a pure (24-karat) "gold" crown at a flea market. After getting it home, she suspends the crown on a scale and finds its weight to be 7.84 N. She then weighs the crown while it is immersed in water and finds that the scale reads 6.86 N. Is the crown made of pure gold? (Similar to Archimedes' problem!)

Solution: Given: $w = 7.84$ N, w (in water) $= 6.86$ N, $\rho_{water} = 1.0 \times 10^3$ kg/m^3.

Find: ρ (density of crown).

There are many different physical quantities we can use to identify matter based on the unique physical quantities of different elements. For example, pure gold and pure aluminum have unique densities, so if we can determine the density of the crown, we can determine whether it is made of pure gold. When the crown is completely submerged in water, the volume of water displaced is equal to the volume of the crown. The "apparent" weight of the crown decreases because the buoyant force cancels part of the crown's true weight. The difference between the true weight and the apparent weight of the crown is therefore the buoyant force,

$F_b = 7.84$ N $- 6.86$ N $= 0.98$ N.

We first find the volume of the crown with Archimedes' principle.

From $F_b = \rho_f V_f g$, we have

$$V_f = \frac{F_b}{\rho_f g} = \frac{0.98 \text{ N}}{(1.0 \times 10^3 \text{ kg/m}^3)(9.80 \text{ m/s}^2)} = 1.00 \times 10^{-4} \text{ m}^3.$$

Now, we can find the density of the crown:

$$\rho = \frac{m}{V} = \frac{w/g}{V} = \frac{w}{gV} = \frac{7.84 \text{ N}}{(9.80 \text{ m/s}^2)(1.00 \times 10^{-4} \text{ m}^3)} = 8.0 \times 10^3 \text{ kg/m}^3.$$

From Table 7.2, we can conclude that this crown is not made of pure gold because the density of gold is 19.3×10^3 kg/m^3, which is much greater than 8.0×10^3 kg/m^3.

---

4.   Fluid Dynamics and Bernoulli's Equation (Section 7.4)

Ideal fluid flow is a steady, irrotational, nonviscous, and incompressible flow. From the conservation of mass, the **equation of continuity** for fluid flow can be derived: ρAv = constant, where ρ is the density of the fluid, A is the cross-sectional area, and v is the speed. If the fluid is incompressible (ρ = constant), then Av = constant, or $A_1 v_1 = A_2 v_2$, which is called the **flow rate equation**, since the quantity, $Q = Av$, measures flow rate, that is volume per unit time. (Can you show that Av has units of m^3/s?)

Bernoulli's equation is the direct result of the application of conservation of energy to fluid. It is written as $p + \frac{1}{2}\rho v^2 + \rho gy = $ constant. If the flow is at a constant height, $y = $ constant, then $p + \frac{1}{2}\rho v^2 = $ constant, that is, "the higher the speed, the lower the pressure, or vice versa." Because speed is related to kinetic energy, and pressure is associated with fluid height and so potential energy, Bernoulli's equation simply is another way of stating that kinetic energy plus potential energy is a constant. This equation successfully explains physical phenomena such as the curve ball in a baseball game.

Example 7.7   An ideal fluid flows at 4.0 m/s in a horizontal circular pipe. If the pipe narrows to half of its original radius, what is the flow speed in the narrow section?

Solution: Given: $v_1 = 4.0$ m/s, $r_2 = r_1/2$.

Find: v_2.

From the flow rate equation, $A_1 v_1 = A_2 v_2$, we have

$$v_2 = \frac{A_1 v_1}{A_2} = \frac{\pi r_1^2 v_1}{\pi r_2^2} = \frac{r_1^2 v_1}{(r_1/2)^2} = \frac{v_1}{1/4} = 4v_1 = 4(4.0 \text{ m/s}) = 16 \text{ m/s}.$$

Note: The pipe narrows to half of its original radius, and the speed increases by a factor of 4. Why?

Example 7.8   In Example 7.7, if the fluid is water and the pressure at the narrow section is 1.8×10^5 Pa, what is the pressure at the wide section?

Solution: Given: $\rho = 1.0 \times 10^3$ kg/m^3, $p_2 = 1.8 \times 10^5$ Pa, $v_1 = 4.0$ m/s, $v_2 = 16$ m/s (Example 9.7).

Find: p_1.

Because the fluid is flowing horizontally, y is constant, so Bernoulli's equation can be written as

$$p_1 + \frac{1}{2}\rho v_1^2 = p_2 + \frac{1}{2}\rho v_2^2;$$

$$p_1 = p_2 + \frac{1}{2}\rho(v_2^2 - v_1^2) = 1.8 \times 10^5 \text{ Pa} + \frac{1}{2}(1.0 \times 10^3 \text{ kg/m}^3)[(16 \text{ m/s})^2 - (4.0 \text{ m/s})^2] = 3.0 \times 10^5 \text{ Pa}.$$

Note: The speed is lower but the pressure is higher in the wide section.

---

*5.   Surface Tension; Viscosity and Poiseuille's Law (Section 7.5)

The **surface tension** of a liquid is caused by the inward pull on the surface molecules, which causes the surface of the liquid to contract and be stretched. The **Coefficient of viscosity** (or **viscosity**), η, is a measure of the fluid's internal resistance to flow.

The average **flow rate**, $Q = Av$ (volume/time, m^3/s), depends on the characteristics of the fluid and the pipe as well as on the pressure difference between the ends of the pipe. **Poiseuille's law** gives a relationship for the flow rate, $Q = \dfrac{\pi r^4 \Delta p}{8 \eta L}$, where r is the radius of the pipe, L its length, Δp the pressure difference between the ends of the pipe, and η the viscosity of the fluid. An interesting result is that the flow rate is proportional to r^4, that is, doubling the radius of a pipe can increase the flow rate by $2^4 = 16$ times.

III. Mathematical Summary

Stress	$\text{stress} = \dfrac{F}{A}$ $\quad(7.1)$	Defines stress.
Strain (tensile)	$\text{strain} = \dfrac{|\Delta L|}{L_o} = \dfrac{|L - L_o|}{L_o}$ $\quad(7.2)$	Defines tensile strain.
Young's Modulus	$Y = \dfrac{F/A}{\Delta L/L_o}$ $\quad(7.4)$	Relates Young's modulus with stress and strain.
Shear Modulus	$S = \dfrac{F/A}{x/h} \approx \dfrac{F/A}{\phi}$ $\quad(7.5)$	Relates shear modulus with stress and shear strain.
Bulk Modulus	$B = \dfrac{F/A}{-\Delta V/V_o} = -\dfrac{\Delta p}{\Delta V/V_o}$ $\quad(7.6)$	Relates bulk modulus with stress and volume strain.
Pressure	$p = \dfrac{F}{A}$ $\quad(7.8a)$	Defines pressure in terms of force and area.
Pressure-Depth Equation	$p = p_o + \rho g h$ $\quad(7.10)$	Expresses pressure as a function of depth in fluid.
Archimedes' Principle	$F_b = m_f g = \rho_f g V_f$ $\quad(7.14)$	Calculates buoyant force.
Equation of Continuity	$\rho_1 A_1 v_1 = \rho_2 A_2 v_2$ or $\rho A v = \text{constant}$ $\quad(7.16)$	Relates flow characteristics for ideal fluid.
Flow Rate Equation	$A_1 v_1 = A_2 v_2$ or $A v = \text{constant}$ $\quad(7.17)$	Rewrites equation of continuity for an incompressible fluid.
Bernoulli's Equation	$p_1 + \frac{1}{2}\rho v_1^2 + \rho g y_1$ $= p_2 + \frac{1}{2}\rho v_2^2 + \rho g y_2$ or $p + \frac{1}{2}\rho v^2 + \rho g y = \text{constant}$ $\quad(7.18)$	Applies the conservation of energy to a fluid.
*Poiseuille's Law	$Q = \dfrac{\pi r^4 \Delta p}{8 \eta L}$ $\quad(7.19)$	Relates the flow rate to fluid characteristics.

IV. Solutions of Selected Exercises and Paired Exercises

10. From the definition of Young's modulus, $Y = \dfrac{F/A}{\Delta L / L_0} = \dfrac{F L_0}{A \Delta L}$, we have

$$\Delta L = \frac{F L_0}{Y A} = \frac{(5.0 \text{ kg})(9.80 \text{ m/s}^2)(2.0 \text{ m})}{(7.0 \times 10^{10} \text{ N/m}^2)(\pi)(1.0 \times 10^{-3} \text{ m})^2} = 4.5 \times 10^{-4} \text{ m} = \boxed{0.45 \text{ mm}}.$$

17. From the definition of shear modulus, we have

$$S = \frac{\text{stress}}{\text{strain}} = \frac{F/A}{x/h} = \frac{Fh}{Ax} = \frac{(0.40 \text{ N})(0.040 \text{ m})}{(0.10 \text{ m})(0.080 \text{ m})(0.30 \times 10^{-3} \text{ m})} = \boxed{6.7 \times 10^3 \text{ N/m}^2}.$$

32. (a) $p_w = \rho g h = (1000 \text{ kg/m}^3)(9.80 \text{ m/s}^2)(15 \text{ m}) = \boxed{1.5 \times 10^5 \text{ Pa}}.$

    (b) $p = p_0 + p_w = 1.01 \times 10^5 \text{ Pa} + 1.5 \times 10^5 \text{ Pa} = \boxed{2.5 \times 10^5 \text{ Pa}}.$

38. The pressure decrease is $\Delta p = \rho g h = (1.29 \text{ kg/m}^3)(9.80 \text{ m/s}^2)(35 \text{ m}) = 442 \text{ Pa}$,

    so the fractional decrease is $\dfrac{\Delta p}{p_a} = \dfrac{442 \text{ Pa}}{1.013 \times 10^5 \text{ Pa}} = 4.37 \times 10^{-3} = \boxed{0.44\%}.$

41. The net force due to air pressure is

$$F_{net} = (\Delta p)A = (1.01 \times 10^5 \text{ Pa} - 2.7 \times 10^4 \text{ Pa})(3.0 \text{ m}^2) = \boxed{2.2 \times 10^5 \text{ N (about 50 000 lb)}}.$$

44. (a) From Pascal's principle, $p_i = p_0 = \dfrac{F_0}{A_0} = \dfrac{1.5 \times 10^6 \text{ N}}{0.20 \text{ m}^2} = \boxed{7.5 \times 10^6 \text{ Pa}}.$

    (b) $F_i = P_i A_i = (7.5 \times 10^6 \text{ Pa})(\pi)(0.025 \text{ m})^2 = \boxed{1.5 \times 10^4 \text{ N}}.$

56. (a) The object will $\boxed{\text{stay at any height}}$ because the weight is exactly balanced by the buoyant force.

    Wherever the object is placed, it stays at that place.

    (b) $F_b = \rho_f g V_f = (1000 \text{ kg/m}^3)(9.80 \text{ m/s}^2)(0.085 \text{ m})^3 = 6.02 \text{ N}$,

    and $W = mg = (0.65 \text{ kg})(9.80 \text{ m/s}^2) = 6.37 \text{ N}$. Because $W > F_b$, the object will $\boxed{\text{sink}}$.

60. First find the volume of the crown with buoyancy.

    $F_b = 8.0 \text{ N} - 4.0 \text{ N} = 4.0 \text{ N} = \rho_f g V_f$,

    so $V = \dfrac{F_b}{\rho_f g} = \dfrac{4.0 \text{ N}}{(1000 \text{ kg/m}^3)(9.80 \text{ m/s}^2)} = 4.08 \times 10^{-4} \text{ m}^3.$

    $\rho = \dfrac{m}{V} = \dfrac{w/g}{V} = \dfrac{8.0 \text{ N}}{(9.80 \text{ m/s}^2)(4.08 \times 10^{-4} \text{ m}^3)} = \boxed{2.0 \times 10^3 \text{ kg/m}^3}.$

64. For the hollow cube to float, its weight has to be balanced by the buoyant force:

$w = mg = (\rho V)F_b = \rho_f g V_f = \rho_f g L^3$, where ρ is density of the cube (iron), V is the volume of the solid cube, and V_f the volume of the hollow cube.

Thus, $L = \sqrt[3]{\dfrac{m}{\rho_f}} = \sqrt[3]{\dfrac{\rho V}{\rho_f}} = \sqrt[3]{\dfrac{(7.8\times10^3 \text{ kg/m}^3)(1.0 \text{ m})^3}{1000 \text{ kg/m}^3}} = \boxed{2.0 \text{ m}}$.

67. Assume the volume of the oak is V. Then its mass is $m = \rho_{oak}V$.

$\Sigma F = F_b - w = \rho_{water}gV - mg = \rho_{water}gV - \rho_{oak}gV = (\rho_{water} - \rho_{oak})gV$.

From Newton's second law, we have

$a = \dfrac{\Sigma F}{m} = \dfrac{(\rho_{water} - \rho_{oak})gV}{\rho_{oak} V} = \dfrac{\rho_{water} - \rho_{oak}}{\rho_{oak}}g = \dfrac{1000 \text{ kg/m}^3 - 810 \text{ kg/m}^3}{810 \text{ kg/m}^3}(9.80 \text{ m/s}^2) = \boxed{2.3 \text{ m/s}^2}$.

76. From the flow rate equation, $A_1v_1 = A_2v_2$, we have

$v_2 = \dfrac{A_1}{A_2}v_1 = \dfrac{\pi(0.20 \text{ m})^2}{\pi(0.35 \text{ m})^2} \times (3.0 \text{ m/s}) = \boxed{0.98 \text{ m/s}}$.

79. (a) The flow rate is $Q = Av = \pi(0.50 \text{ cm})^2(4.5 \text{ cm/s}) = \boxed{3.5 \text{ cm}^3/\text{s}}$.

(b) From the flow rate equation, we know that $Q = Av$ is a constant,

so the speed in the capillaries is $v = \dfrac{Q}{A} = \dfrac{3.53 \text{ cm}^3/\text{s}}{2500 \text{ cm}^2} = 1.41 \times 10^{-3} \text{ cm/s}$.

Therefore, the percentage is $\dfrac{1.41 \times 10^{-3} \text{ cm/s}}{4.5 \text{ cm/s}} = 3.1 \times 10^{-4} = \boxed{0.031\%}$.

(c) It is a physiological need. The slow speed is needed to allow for the exchange of substances such as oxygen between the blood and the tissues.

83. The flow rate is $Q = A_1v_1$,

so $v_1 = \dfrac{Q}{A_1} = \dfrac{(25 \text{ L/min})(10^{-3} \text{ m}^3/\text{L})(1 \text{ min}/60 \text{ s})}{\pi(0.035 \text{ m})^2} = 0.108 \text{ m/s}$.

From the flow rate equation, $A_1v_1 = A_2v_2$, we have

$v_2 = \dfrac{A_1v_1}{A_2} = \dfrac{\pi(0.035 \text{ m})^2(0.108 \text{ m/s})}{(30 \text{ cm}^2)(10^{-4} \text{ m}^2/\text{cm}^2)} = 0.139 \text{ m/s}$.

Then, we use Bernoulli's principle, $p_1 + \frac{1}{2}\rho v_1^2 + \rho gy_1 = p_2 + \frac{1}{2}\rho v_2^2 + \rho gy_2$.

With $y_1 = y_2$, we have

$p_2 = p_1 + \frac{1}{2}\rho(v_1^2 - v_2^2) = 6.0 \text{ Pa} + \frac{1}{2}(1000 \text{ kg/m}^3)[(0.108 \text{ m/s})^2 - (0.139 \text{ m/s})^2] = \boxed{2.2 \text{ Pa}}$.

93. (a) The weight is balanced by the buoyant force:

$$w = mg = F_b = \rho_f g V, \quad \text{so} \quad V = \frac{m}{\rho_f} = \frac{\rho V}{\rho_f} = \frac{(700 \text{ kg/m}^3)(0.30 \text{ m})^3}{1000 \text{ kg/m}^3} = 0.0189 \text{ m}^3.$$

Thus, the distance from the top of the wood to the water surface is

$$0.30 \text{ m} - \frac{0.0189 \text{ m}^3}{(0.30 \text{ m})(0.30 \text{ m})} = \boxed{0.09 \text{ m}}.$$

(b) The 0.09 m above the water surface can support the mass on top of the wood.

The mass is $\dfrac{(1000 \text{ kg/m}^3)(0.30 \text{ m})^2(0.09 \text{ m})g}{g} = \boxed{8.1 \text{ kg}}.$

97. The pressure of the oil is $p_o = \rho_o g h_o = \rho_m g h_m$,

so $\quad \rho_o = \dfrac{\rho_m h_m}{h_o} = \dfrac{(13.6 \times 10^3 \text{ kg/m}^3)(5.0 \text{ cm})}{80 \text{ cm}} = \boxed{8.5 \times 10^2 \text{ kg/m}^3}.$

V. Practice Quiz

1. What is the gauge pressure at the bottom of a 5.0-m-deep swimming pool?

   (a) 4.9×10^4 Pa   (b) 7.2×10^4 Pa   (c) 1.01×10^5 Pa   (d) 1.5×10^5 Pa   (e) 2.51×10^5 Pa

2. A string supports a 4.00-kg cylinder made of solid iron while submerged in water. What is the tension in the string? (The density of iron is 7.86×10^3 kg/m^3.)

   (a) 0 N   (b) 2.50 N   (c) 19.6 N   (d) 23.7 N   (e) 34.2 N

3. When you turn on a showerhead quickly, you notice that the shower curtain moves inward. This is because

   (a) the air inside the curtain moves faster, and the pressure is higher.

   (b) the air inside the curtain moves faster, and the pressure is lower.

   (c) the air inside the curtain moves slower, and the pressure is lower.

   (d) the air inside the curtain moves slower, and the pressure is higher.

   (e) None of the preceding applies.

4. An ideal fluid flows through a pipe made of two sections with diameters of 2.0 and 6.0 cm, respectively. What is the speed ratio of the flow through the 2.0-cm section to that through the 6.0-cm section?

   (a) 1/9   (b) 1/3   (c) 1   (d) 3   (e) 9

5. A 25 000-N truck on a hydraulic lift rests on a cylinder with a piston of diameter 0.40 m. What is the minimum pressure that must be applied to the hydraulic liquid in order to lift the car?

   (a) 2.0×10^4 N/m^2 (b) 4.0×10^4 N/m^2 (c) 5.0×10^4 N/m^2 (d) 1.6×10^5 N/m^2 (e) 2.0×10^5 N/m^2

6. Which of the following is associated with the law of conservation of energy for fluids?

(a) Archimedes' principle   (b) Bernoulli's principle   (c) Pascal's principle

(d) Poiseuille's law   (e) equation of continuity

7. The same object is hung from identical wires made of aluminum, brass, copper, and steel. Which wire will stretch the least?

(a) aluminum   (b) brass   (c) copper   (d) steel   (e) All will stretch the same.

8. Water flows with a speed of 8.0 m/s in a horizontal pipe 2.0 cm in diameter. The water then enters a horizontal pipe 4.0 cm in diameter. What is the difference in pressure between the two segments?

(a) 1.0×10^4 N/m^2 (b) 2.0×10^4 N/m^2 (c) 3.0×10^4 N/m^2 (d) 4.0×10^4 N/m^2 (e) 5.0×10^4 N/m^2

9. In a gasoline spill, a gasoline layer 0.50 cm thick was found above a surface. Estimate the gauge pressure of the gasoline.

(a) 0.33 N/m^2 (b) 3.3 N/m^2 (c) 33 N/m^2 (d) 3.3×10^2 N/m^2 (e) 3.3×10^3 N/m^2

10. If the density of gold is 19.3×10^3 kg/m^3, what buoyant force does a 0.60-kg gold crown experience when it is immersed in water?

(a) 3.0×10^{-5} N   (b) 3.0×10^{-4} N   (c) 3.0×10^{-2} N   (d) 0.30 N   (e) 3.0 N

11. A 500-N shear force is applied to one face of an iron cube measuring 10 cm on each side. What is the displacement of that face relative to the opposite face?

(a) 6.1×10^{-5} m   (b) 6.1×10^{-6} m   (c) 6.1×10^{-7} m   (d) 6.1×10^{-8} m   (e) 6.1×10^{-9} m

12. An object floats in a freshwater lake with 60% of its body beneath the surface of the water. What is the density of the object?

(a) 400 kg/m^3 (b) 500 kg/m^3 (c) 600 kg/m^3 (d) 980 kg/m^3 (e) 1000 kg/m^3

Answers to Practice Quiz:

1. a 2. e 3. b 4. e 5. a 6. b 7. d 8. c 9. c 10. d 11. d 12. c

CHAPTER 8

Temperature and Kinetic Theory

I.   Chapter Objectives

Upon completion of this chapter, you should be able to:

1.   distinguish between temperature and heat.

2.   explain how a temperature scale is constructed and convert temperatures from one scale to another.

3.   describe the ideal gas law, explain how it is used to determine absolute zero, and understand the kelvin temperature scale.

4.   understand and calculate the thermal expansions of solids and liquids.

5.   relate kinetic theory and temperature, and explain the process of diffusion.

*6.   understand the difference between monatomic and diatomic gases, the meaning of the equipartition theorem, and the expression for the internal energy of a diatomic gas.

II.   Chapter Summary and Discussion

1.   Temperature and Heat (Section 8.1)

Temperature is a relative measure, or indication, of hotness and coldness. The result of the kinetic theory of gases states that temperature is a measure of the average kinetic energy of the molecules.

Heat is the net energy transferred from one object to another because of a temperature difference. The total energy (kinetic plus potential) of all molecules of a body or system is the **internal energy**. When heat is transferred out of or into a system in the absence of any other physical process, the internal energy of the system will change.

Note: If a system has a higher temperature, it does not necessarily mean that the system has a greater internal energy than another. The number of molecules is also a factor in determining the internal energy of a system.

When heat is transferred between two objects, whether or not they are physically touching, they are said to be in **thermal contact**. When there is no longer a net heat transfer between objects in thermal contact, they are at the same temperature and are said to be in **thermal equilibrium**.

2. The Celsius and Fahrenheit Temperature Scales (Section 8.2)

The two most common temperature scales are the **Celsius temperature scale** and the **Fahrenheit temperature scale**. On the Celsius scale, water freezes at 0°C and boils at 100°C, whereas on the Fahrenheit scale, water freezes at 32°F and boils at 212°F. The conversions between the two scales are

$$T_F = \tfrac{9}{5}T_C + 32, \text{ or } T_C = \tfrac{5}{9}(T_F - 32).$$

Note: To convert T_C to T_F, you need to multiply by $\tfrac{9}{5}$ and then add 32; however, to convert T_F to T_C, you need to subtract 32 and then multiply by $\tfrac{5}{9}$.

When a temperature difference or change is mentioned, the notation is C° rather than °C for a particular temperature. For example, we say "today's temperature is 20°C, but the change in temperature between today and yesterday is 10 C°."

Example 8.1   What is the temperature 50.0°F on the Celsius scale?

Solution: Given: $T_F = 50.0°F$.   Find: T_C.

$T_C = \tfrac{5}{9}(T_F - 32) = \tfrac{5}{9}(50 - 32) = 10°C.$

Example 8.2   The temperature changes from 35°F during the night to 75°F during the day. What is the temperature change on the Celsius scale?

Solution: Given: $\Delta T_F = 75°F - 35°F = 40\ F°$. [**Note**: The unit for Fahrenheit temperature change is F° (Fahrenheit degree), not °F (degrees Fahrenheit).]

Find: ΔT_F.

Although we can convert both 35°F and 75°F to their Celsius temperatures and then calculate the change, we can take advantage of the conversion equations to calculate the temperature change, ΔT.

From $T_C = \tfrac{5}{9}(T_F - 32)$, we can see that for every Fahrenheit degree increase, the Celsius temperature increases by $\tfrac{5}{9}$ degree, or $\Delta T_C = \tfrac{5}{9}\Delta T_F$.

Thus, $\Delta T_C = \tfrac{5}{9}\Delta T_F = \tfrac{5}{9}(40) = 22\ C°$. (**Note**: The unit for Celsius temperature change is C°, not °C.)

---

3. Gas Law and Absolute Temperature (Section 8.3)

An ideal gas is a low-density, low-pressure gas. The **ideal** (or perfect) **gas law** relates the pressure, volume and temperature of the gas, $pV = Nk_B T$, where N is the number of molecules and k_B is the Boltzmann constant, which has a value of 1.38×10^{-23} J/K. It describes real, low-density gases fairly well. Two other forms of the ideal gas law are $pV = nRT$ (macroscopic form) and $\dfrac{p_1 V_1}{T_1} = \dfrac{p_2 V_2}{T_2}$, where n is the number of moles of molecules, and R is the universal gas constant, which has a value of 8.31 J/(mol·K). One mole of substance is defined as containing $N_A = 6.02 \times 10^{23}$ molecules (Avogadro's number).

A gas can be used to measure temperature as a function of time at a constant volume. Extrapolation to zero pressure defines absolute zero temperature. **Absolute zero** is the foundation for the **Kelvin temperature scale**, which uses absolute zero and the **triple point of water** as fixed points. The conversion between Kelvin and Celsius temperatures is $T_K = T_C + 273.15$, or more commonly to three significant figures, $T_K = T_C + 273$.

Note: The temperature in the ideal gas law *must* be the Kelvin temperature.

Example 8.3   What is –40°F on the Kelvin scale?

Solution: Given: $T_F = -40°C$.   Find: T_K.

Since there is no direct conversion given between Fahrenheit and Kelvin temperatures, we first convert Fahrenheit to Celsius.

$T_C = \frac{5}{9}(T_F - 32) = \frac{5}{9}(-40 - 32) = \frac{5}{9}(-72) = -40°C$.

(Wow! The Celsius and Fahrenheit are nominally the same readings at this temperature.)

Next, $T_K = T_C + 273 = -40 + 273 = 233$ K.

Example 8.4   A gas has a volume of 0.20 m³, a temperature of 30°C, and a pressure of 1.0 atm (one atmosphere of pressure). It is heated to 60°C and compressed to a volume of 0.15 m³. Find the new pressure in atmospheres.

Solution: Given: $T_1 = 30°C$, $V_1 = 0.20$ m³, $p_1 = 1.0$ atm,

$T_2 = 60°C$, $V_2 = 0.15$ m².

Find: p_2 (in atm).

The temperatures are given on the Celsius scale, so we first convert them to Kelvin temperatures.

$T_1 = 30°C = 30 + 273 = 303$ K, and $T_2 = 60°C = 60 + 273 = 333$ K.

From $\dfrac{p_1 V_1}{T_1} = \dfrac{p_2 V_2}{T_2}$, we have $p_2 = \dfrac{V_1}{V_2} \times \dfrac{T_2}{T_1} \times p_1 = \dfrac{0.20 \text{ m}^3}{0.15 \text{ m}^2} \times \dfrac{333 \text{ K}}{303 \text{ K}} \times (1.0 \text{ atm}) = 1.5$ atm.

Note: Leaving the pressure in units of atm gives the new pressure also in atm because of the ratio form of the ideal gas law. Also, the temperatures used in the ideal gas law *must* be the Kelvin temperatures. What would happen if you used a temperature of $T_1 = 0°C$ in the example?

Example 8.5   An ideal gas in a 1000-cm^3 (1 liter) container has a pressure of 1.00×10^4 N/m^2 at 20.0°C. Determine the number of gas molecules and the number of moles of gas in the container.

Solution: Given: $V = 1000$ cm^3, $T = 20.0°C$, $p = 1.00 \times 10^4$ N/m^2.

Find: N and n.

The volume is not given in m^3 (the standard SI unit), so we first need to convert the volume to m^3 and temperature to Kelvin. Although 1 m = 100 cm, 1 m$^3 \neq$ 100 cm^3.

Actually 1 m^3 = (1 m)^3 = (100 cm)^3 = 10^6 cm^3.

$V = (1000 \text{ cm}^3) \times \dfrac{1 \text{ m}^3}{10^6 \text{ cm}^3} = 1.00 \times 10^{-3}$ m^3.

$T = T_C + 273 = 20.0 + 273 = 293$ K.

From $pV = Nk_B T$, $N = \dfrac{pV}{k_B T} = \dfrac{(1.00 \times 10^4 \text{ N/m}^2)(1.00 \times 10^{-3} \text{ m}^3)}{(1.38 \times 10^{-23} \text{ J/K})(293 \text{ K})} = 2.47 \times 10^{21}$ molecules.

$n = \dfrac{N}{N_A} = \dfrac{2.47 \times 10^{21} \text{ molecules}}{6.02 \times 10^{23} \text{ molecues/mol}} = 4.10 \times 10^{-3}$ mol.

---

4.   Thermal Expansion (Section 8.4)

The **thermal expansion** of a material is characterized by its coefficient of expansion. For solids, the **thermal coefficient of linear expansion**, α, applies to one-dimensional length changes; the **thermal coefficient of area expansion** (approximately equal to 2α) applies to two-dimensional area changes; and the **thermal coefficient of volume expansion** (approximately equal to 3α) applies to three-dimensional volume changes. For fluids with no definite shape, only volume expansion is applicable, and a special thermal coefficient of volume expansion β is used. We use the following equations to calculate the thermal expansions:

Linear:	$\dfrac{\Delta L}{L_0} = \alpha \Delta T$	Area:	$\dfrac{\Delta A}{A_0} = 2\alpha \Delta T$
Volume:	$\dfrac{\Delta V}{V_0} = 3\alpha \Delta T$ (for solids)	Volume:	$\dfrac{\Delta V}{V_0} = \beta \Delta T$ (for fluids)

Example 8.6 You are installing some outdoor copper electric wire to a backyard fish pond on a hot 40°C summer day. The temperature could be as low as –20°C in your area during a cold winter night. How much extra wire (minimum) do you have to include allowing for thermal expansion if the distance from the electric service to the pond is 100 m?

Solution: Given: $L_0 = 100$ m, $T_i = 40°C$, $T_f = -20°C$, $\alpha = 17 \times 10^{-6}$ /C° (from Table 10.1).

Find: ΔL.

If you cut the wire exactly 100 m in the summer, then it will shrink to a length shorter than 100 m in the winter, and the wire will snap. Thus, we want to make sure that the wire is at least 100 m long during the winter and calculate the corresponding length in the summer.

$\Delta T = T_f - T_i = -20°C - (40°C) = -60$ C°.

From $\dfrac{\Delta L}{L_0} = \alpha \Delta T$, we have $\Delta L = \alpha \Delta T L_0 = (17 \times 10^{-6}$ /C°$)(-60$ C°$)(100$ m$) = -0.10$ m.

Here, the negative sign simply means that the result is a compression (negative expansion).

Example 8.7 A 500-mL glass beaker of water is filled to the rim at a temperature of 0°C. How much water will overflow if the water is heated to a temperature of 95°C? (Ignore the expansion of the beaker. Why?)

Solution: Given: $V_0 = 500$ mL, $T_i = 0°C$, $T_f = 95°C$, $\beta = 2.1 \times 10^{-4}$ /C° (from Table 10.1).

Find: ΔV.

$\Delta T = T_f - T_i = 95°C - 0°C = 95$ C°.

The amount of water that overflows is simply equal to the change in volume of the water.

From $\dfrac{\Delta V}{V_0} = \beta \Delta T$, we have $\Delta V = \beta \Delta T V_0 = (2.1 \times 10^{-4}$ /C°$)(95$ C°$)(500$ mL$) = 10$ mL.

Note: In this example, we can ignore the expansion of the beaker because glass has a much smaller coefficient of volume expansion (approximately $3\beta = 10 \times 10^{-6}$ /C° $<< 2.1 \times 10^{-4}$ /C°).

---

5. The Kinetic Theory of Gases (Section 8.5)

The **kinetic theory of gases** uses statistical methods to derive the ideal gas law from mechanical principles. Some of the important conclusions of this theory as follows:

(1)   Temperature is a measure of the average kinetic energy of the molecules, $\frac{1}{2}mv_{rms}^2 = \frac{3}{2}k_B T$, where v_{rms} is the root-mean-square (rms) speed of the molecules, and m is the mass of the molecule.

(2)   The ideal gas law can be expressed in terms of the root-mean-square speed of the molecules,

$$pV = \frac{1}{3}Nmv_{rms}^2.$$

(3)   The total internal energy of an ideal monatomic gas is given by $U = \frac{3}{2}Nk_B T = \frac{3}{2}nRT$.

Diffusion is a process of random molecular mixing in which particular molecules move from a region of higher concentration to one of lower concentration. **Osmosis** is the diffusion of a liquid across a permeable membrane because of a concentration gradient (difference).

Example 8.8   Calculate the rms speed of a hydrogen molecule and of an oxygen molecule at a temperature of 300 K. (The masses of hydrogen and oxygen molecules are 3.3×10^{-27} kg and 5.3×10^{-26} kg, respectively.)

Solution: Given: $T = 300$ K, $m_H = 3.3 \times 10^{-27}$ kg, $m_O = 5.3 \times 10^{-26}$ kg.

Find: v_{rms} for H_2 and O_2.

From $\frac{1}{2}mv_{rms}^2 = \frac{3}{2}k_B T$, we have $v_{rms} = \sqrt{\dfrac{3k_B T}{m}}$.

For H_2: $v_{rms} = \sqrt{\dfrac{3(1.38 \times 10^{-23}\ \text{J/K})(300\ \text{K})}{3.3 \times 10^{-27}\ \text{kg}}} = 1.9 \times 10^3$ m/s (about 4000 mi/h).

For O_2: $v_{rms} = \sqrt{\dfrac{3(1.38 \times 10^{-23}\ \text{J/K})(300\ \text{K})}{5.3 \times 10^{-26}\ \text{kg}}} = 4.8 \times 10^2$ m/s.

Why does the gas with the more massive molecule have a smaller v_{rms}?

Example 8.9   If the temperature of a gas increases from 20°C to 40°C, by what factor does the rms speed increase?

Solution: Given: $T_1 = 20°C = 20 + 273 = 293$ K, $T_2 = 40°C = 40 + 273 = 313$ K.

(The temperatures *must* be Kelvin!)

Find: $\dfrac{(v_{rms})_2}{(v_{rms})_1}$.

From $\frac{1}{2}mv_{rms}^2 = \frac{3}{2}k_B T$, we have $v_{rms} = \sqrt{\dfrac{3k_B T}{m}}$.

Thus, $\dfrac{(v_{rms})_2}{(v_{rms})_1} = \sqrt{\dfrac{T_2}{T_1}} = \sqrt{\dfrac{313 \text{ K}}{293 \text{ K}}} = 1.03$,   or it increases by only 3%.

Note: Because k_B and m are constant, they cancel in the ratio $\dfrac{(v_{rms})_2}{(v_{rms})_1}$. The Celsius temperature doubles in this example, but the rms speed does not double (it increases by only 3%), nor does the Kelvin temperature.

---

*6.   Kinetic Theory, Diatomic Gases, and the Equipartition Theorem (Section 8.6)

For monatomic gases, the total internal energy, U, consists solely of translational kinetic energy because a monatomic molecule cannot rotate; however, diatomic molecules can rotate, so the kinetic energy associated with these motions should also be included. The average translational kinetic energy of any molecule is always equal to $\frac{1}{2}mv_{rms}^2 = \frac{3}{2}k_B T$.

A monatomic molecule has three independent ways of possessing kinetic energy: with x, y, or z linear motion. A diatomic molecule has three independent ways of possessing translational kinetic energy and two independent ways of possessing rotational kinetic energy. Each independent way of possessing energy is called a **degree of freedom**.

The **equipartition theorem** states: On average, the total internal energy (U) of an ideal gas is divided equally among the degrees of freedom its molecules possess. Furthermore, each degree of freedom contributes $\frac{1}{2}Nk_B T$ (or $\frac{1}{2}nRT$) to the total internal energy.

According to this theorem, a monatomic gas possesses $3(\frac{1}{2}Nk_B T) = \frac{3}{2}Nk_B T$ (or $\frac{3}{2}nRT$) of internal energy because it has three degrees of freedom, and a diatomic gas possesses $5(\frac{1}{2}Nk_B T) = \frac{5}{2}Nk_B T$ (or $\frac{5}{2}nRT$) of internal energy because it has five degrees of freedom. Of the $\frac{5}{2}Nk_B T$ internal energy for a diatomic gas, $\frac{3}{2}Nk_B T$ is from translational motion, and $\frac{2}{2}Nk_B T$ is from rotational motion. (A diatomic molecule has a vibrational degree of freedom as well; however, the contribution from vibration at room temperature is negligible compared with total internal energy.)

III. Mathematical Summary

Celsius—Fahrenheit Conversion	$T_F = \frac{9}{5}T_C + 32$ (8.1) $T_C = \frac{5}{9}(T_F - 32)$ (8.2)	Converts between Celsius and Fahrenheit temperature scales.
Ideal (or perfect) Gas Law (always absolute temperature)	$\frac{p_1 V_1}{T_1} = \frac{p_2 V_2}{T_2}$ (8.5) or $pV = Nk_B T$ (8.6) or or $pV = nRT$ (8.7)	Relates pressure, volume, and absolute temperature. $k_B = 1.38 \times 10^{-23}$ J/K $R = 8.31$ J/(mol·K) Avogadro's number: $N_A = 6.02 \times 10^{23}$ molecules/mole
Kelvin—Celsius Conversion	$T_K = T_C + 273$ (8.8a)	Converts between Celsius and Kelvin temperature scales.
Thermal Expansion of Solids: Linear	$\frac{\Delta L}{L_0} = \alpha \Delta T$ (8.9) or $L = L_0(1 + \alpha \Delta T)$ (8.10)	Calculates the fractional change in length in terms of the coefficient of linear expansion and change in temperature.
Thermal Expansion of Solids: Area	$\frac{\Delta A}{A_0} = 2\alpha \Delta T$ or $A = A_0(1 + 2\alpha \Delta T)$ (8.11)	Calculates the fractional change in area in terms of the coefficient of linear expansion and change in temperature.
Thermal Expansion of Solids: Volume	$\frac{\Delta V}{V_0} = 3\alpha \Delta T$ or $V = V_0(1 + 3\alpha \Delta T)$ (8.12)	Calculates the fractional change in volume in terms of the coefficient of linear expansion and change in temperature.
Thermal Volume Expansion of Fluids	$\frac{\Delta V}{V_0} = \beta \Delta T$ (8.13)	Calculates the fractional change in volume in terms of the coefficient of volume expansion and change in temperature.
Results of Kinetic Theory of Gases	$pV = \frac{1}{3}Nmv_{rms}^2$ (8.14) $\frac{1}{2}mv_{rms}^2 = \frac{3}{2}k_B T$ (8.15) $U = \frac{3}{2}Nk_B T = \frac{3}{2}nRT$ (8.16) $U = \frac{5}{2}Nk_B T = \frac{5}{2}nRT$ (8.17)	Gives the results of the kinetic theory of gases. Relates absolute temperature to kinetic energy. For ideal monatomic gas only. For diatomic gas only.

IV. Solutions of Selected Exercises and Paired Exercises

10. $T_F = \frac{9}{5}T_C + 32 = \frac{9}{5}(39.4) + 32 = \boxed{103°F}$.

13. $T_F = \frac{9}{5}T_C + 32 = \frac{9}{5}(58) + 32 = \boxed{136°F}$.

    $T_F = \frac{9}{5}(-89) + 32 = \boxed{-128°F}$.

26. (a) $T_K = T_C + 273.15 = 0 + 273.15 = \boxed{273\ K}$.   (b) $T_K = 100 + 273.15 = \boxed{373\ K}$.

    (c) $T_K = 20 + 273.15 = \boxed{293\ K}$.   (d) $T_K = -35 + 273.15 = \boxed{238\ K}$.

34. From the ideal gas law, $pV = nRT$, we have

    $$V = \frac{nRT}{p} = \frac{(1\ \text{mol})[8.31\ /(\text{mol·K})](273\ K)}{1.01 \times 10^5\ \text{Pa}} = \boxed{0.0224\ \text{m}^3 = 22.4\ \text{L}}.$$

38. $T_1 = 92°F = \frac{5}{9}(92 - 32)\ °C = 33.3°C = 306.3\ K$, and $T_2 = 32°F = 0°C = 273\ K$.

    From the ideal gas law, $\dfrac{p_1 V_1}{T_1} = \dfrac{p_2 V_2}{T_2}$, we have

    $$V_2 = \frac{p_1 V_1 T_2}{T_1 p_2} = \frac{(20.0\ \text{lb/in}^2)(0.20\ \text{m}^3)(273\ K)}{(306.3\ K)(14.7\ \text{lb/in}^2)} = \boxed{0.24\ \text{m}^3}.$$

    Here lb/in^2 can be used, since it is in a ratio.

41. (a) With $p = p_0$, the ideal gas law, $\dfrac{p_0 V_0}{T_0} = \dfrac{pV}{T}$, becomes $\dfrac{V}{V_0} = \dfrac{T p_0}{T_0 p} = \dfrac{T}{T_0}$.

    Therefore, the volume of the gas $\boxed{\text{increases}}$ with temperature.

    (b) $\dfrac{V}{V_0} = \dfrac{T}{T_0} = \dfrac{313\ K}{283\ K} = 1.106$.

    Thus, the fractional change is $\dfrac{V - V_0}{V_0} = \dfrac{V}{V_0} - 1 = 0.106 = \boxed{10.6\%}$.

54. Only the higher temperature needs to be considered because the slabs will not touch under the lower temperature.

    $$\Delta L = \alpha L_0 \Delta T = (12 \times 10^{-6}\ \text{C}°^{-1})(10.0\ \text{m})[45°C - (20°C)] = 3.0 \times 10^{-3}\ \text{m} = \boxed{3.0\ \text{mm}}.$$

58.   (a) The hole will ⬛ get larger ⬛ due to expansion.

        (b) $A_o = \pi r^2 = \pi(4.00 \text{ cm})^2 = 50.27 \text{ cm}^2$.

        $\Delta A = 2\alpha A_o \Delta T = 2(24 \times 10^{-6} \text{ C}^{\circ-1})(50.27 \text{ cm}^2)(150°C - 20°C) = 0.314 \text{ cm}^2$.

        Thus, the final area is $50.27 \text{ cm}^2 + 0.314 \text{ cm}^2 = \boxed{50.6 \text{ cm}^2}$.

61.   (a) There will be a gas $\boxed{\text{spill}}$ because the coefficient of volume expansion is greater for gasoline than steel.

        (b) $\Delta V = \beta V_o \Delta T = (9.5 \times 10^{-4} \text{ C}^{\circ-1})(25 \text{ gal})(30°C - 10°C) = \boxed{0.48 \text{ gal}}$.

71.   (a) $K = \frac{3}{2}k_B T = \frac{3}{2}(1.38 \times 10^{-23} \text{ J/K})(293 \text{ K}) = \boxed{6.1 \times 10^{-21} \text{ J}}$.

        (b) $K = \frac{3}{2}(1.38 \times 10^{-23} \text{ J/K})(373 \text{ K}) = \boxed{7.7 \times 10^{-21} \text{ J}}$.

72.   (a) The internal energy will $\boxed{\text{increase by less than a factor of 2}}$, because the internal energy is directly proportional to the Kelvin temperature, and doubling the Celsius temperature will increase but not double the Kelvin temperature.

        (b) From $U = \frac{3}{2}nRT$, we have $\Delta U = \frac{3}{2}nR\Delta T = \frac{3}{2}(2.0 \text{ mol})[8.31 \text{ J/(mol·K)}](40°C - 20°C) = \boxed{5.0 \times 10^2 \text{ J}}$.

77. $25°C = 298 \text{ K}$ and $100°C = 373 \text{ K}$.

        The rms speed of a gas is $v_{rms} = \sqrt{\dfrac{3k_B T}{m_o}}$, or v_{rms} is proportional to $\sqrt{T}$,

        So $\dfrac{(v_{rms})_2}{(v_{rms})_1} = \sqrt{\dfrac{T_2}{T_1}} = \sqrt{\dfrac{373 \text{ K}}{298 \text{ K}}} = \boxed{1.12 \text{ times}}$.

83.   For a diatomic gas, $U = \frac{5}{2}nRT = \frac{5}{2}(1.0 \text{ mol})[8.31 \text{ J/(mol·K)}](293 \text{ K}) = \boxed{6.1 \times 10^3 \text{ J}}$.

95.   (a) From $T_F = \frac{9}{5}T_C + 32$, we can conclude that $\Delta T_F = \frac{9}{5}\Delta T_F = \frac{9}{5}(10) = \boxed{18 \text{ F}°}$.

        (b) $\Delta T_C = \frac{5}{9}\Delta T_F = \frac{5}{9}(10) = \boxed{5.6 \text{ C}°}$.

V. Practice Quiz

1. Nitrogen condenses into a liquid at approximately 77 K. To what temperature, in degrees Fahrenheit, does this correspond?

   (a) −353°F   (b) −321°F   (c) −196°F   (d) −171°F   (e) −139°F

2. An air bubble of volume 1.0 cm³ is released underwater. As it rises to the surface of the water its volume expands. What will be its new volume if its original temperature and pressure are 5.0°C and 1.2 atm, and its final temperature and pressure are 20°C and 1.0 atm?

   (a) 1.1 cm³   (b) 1.3 cm³   (c) 3.3 m³   (d) 4.0 cm³   (e) 4.8 cm³

3. A fixed container holds oxygen and hydrogen gases at the same temperature. Which one of the following statements is correct?

   (a) The oxygen molecules have the greater kinetic energy.

   (b) The hydrogen molecules have the greater kinetic energy.

   (c) The oxygen molecules have the greater speed.

   (d) The hydrogen molecules have the greater speed.

   (e) They have the same speed and kinetic energy.

4. The absolute (Kelvin) temperature of an ideal gas is directly proportional to which of the following properties, when taken as an average, of the molecules of the gas?

   (a) speed   (b) momentum   (c) mass   (d) kinetic energy   (e) potential energy

5. An aluminum beam is 15.0 m long at a temperature of -15°C. What is its expansion when the temperature is 35°C?

   (a) 1.8×10^{-2} m   (b) 9.0×10^{-3} m   (c) 7.2×10^{-3} m   (d) 1.2×10^{-3} m   (e) 3.6×10^{-4} m.

6. An ideal gas sample has a pressure of 2.5 atm, and a volume of 1.0 L at a temperature of 30°C. How many moles of gas are in the sample?

   (a) 9.9×10^{-4} (b) 1.0×10^{-2} (c) 0.10   (d) 1.1   (e) 2.5

7. A brass cube, 10 cm on a side, is heated with a temperature change of 200 C°. By what percentage docs its volume change?

   (a) 5.7×10^{-3} %   (b) 0.57 %   (c) 1.1 %   (d) 1.1×10^{-3} %   (e) 0.10 %

8. When water warms from 0°C to 4°C, the density of the water

(a) increases. (b) decreases. (c) remains constant.

(d) becomes zero. (e) none of the preceding

9. A molecule has an rms speed of 500 m/s at 20°C. What is its rms speed at 80°C?

(a) 500 m/s (b) 1000 m/s (c) 2000 m/s (d) 550 m/s (e) 600 m/s

10. If one mole of a monatomic gas has a total internal energy of 3.7×10^3 J, what is the total internal energy of one mole of diatomic gas at the same temperature?

(a) zero (b) 2.2×10^3 J (c) 6.2×10^3 J (d) 1.1×10^4 J (e) 1.9×10^4 J

11. The high and low temperatures on a particular day are 25°C and 13°C, respectively. What is that day's temperature change on the Fahrenheit scale?

(a) 6.7 F° (b) 12 F° (c) 22 F° (d) 39 F° (e) 285 F°

12. A radial tire is inflated to a gauge pressure of 35 lb/in^2 at 60°F. If the temperature increases to 100°F while the volume of the tire remains constant, what is the tire's new pressure?

(a) 35 lb/in^2 (b) 38 lb/in^2 (c) 39 lb/in^2 (d) 50 lb/in^2 (e) 54 lb/in^2

Answers to Practice Quiz:

1. b 2. b 3. d 4. d 5. a 6. c 7. d 8. a 9. d 10. c 11. c 12. c

CHAPTER 9

Sound

I. Chapter Objectives

Upon completion of this chapter, you should be able to:

1. define sound and explain the sound frequency spectrum.

2. tell how the speed of sound differs in different media and describe the temperature dependence of the speed of sound in air.

3. define sound intensity and explain how it varies with distance from a point source, and calculate sound intensity levels on the decibel scale.

4. explain the reflection, refraction, and diffraction of sound, and distinguish between constructive and destructive interference.

5. describe and explain the Doppler effect and give some examples of its occurrences and applications.

6. explain some of the sound characteristics of musical instruments in physical terms.

II. Chapter Summary and Discussion

1. Sound Waves (Section 9.1)

Sound waves in fluids are primarily longitudinal waves (or compressional waves). The high- and low-density pressure regions (analogous to crests and troughs of transverse wave) of a sound wave are called *condensations* and *rarefactions*, respectively. All sound waves are produced by vibrating sources such as the human vocal cords.

The **sound frequency spectrum** consists of three regions: frequencies lower than 20 Hz ($f < 20$ Hz) are in the **infrasonic region**, frequencies between about 20 Hz and 20 kHz (20 Hz $< f < 20$ kHz) are in the **audible region**, and frequencies above 20 kHz ($f > 20$ kHz) are in the **ultrasonic region**.

Only sound waves in the audible region with sufficient intensity can initiate nerve impulses (in the ears) that are interpreted by human brains as sound; however, animals such as dolphins and elephants can detect sound waves outside the audible region.

2. The Speed of Sound (Section 9.2)

The **speed of sound** in a particular medium depends on the elasticity or the intermolecular interactions of the medium and the mass or density of its particles. Generally, the speed of sound in solids and liquids is given by

$v = \sqrt{\dfrac{Y}{\rho}}$ and $v = \sqrt{\dfrac{B}{\rho}}$, respectively, where Y is the Young's modulus, B is the bulk modulus, and ρ is the density.

At *normal environmental temperatures*, the speed of sound in air increases by about 0.6 m/s for each Celsius degree above 0°C. A good approximation is given by $v = (331 + 0.6T_C)$ m/s, where T_C is the air temperature in degrees Celsius, and 331 m/s is the speed of sound in air at 0°C. A useful general value for the speed of sound in air is $\frac{1}{3}$ km/s (or $\frac{1}{5}$ mi/s).

Example 9.1   The speed of an ultrasonic sound of frequency 45 kHz in air is 342 m/s.

   (a) What is the air temperature?

   (b) What is the wavelength of the sound wave?

Solution: Given: $v = 342$ m/s, $f = 45$ kHz $= 45 \times 10^3$ Hz.

   Find: (a) T_C (b) λ.

(a) From $v = (331 + 0.6T_C)$ m/s, we have

$$T_C = \frac{v - 331}{0.6} = \frac{342 - 331}{0.6} = 18°C.$$

(b) Because $v = \lambda f$, $\lambda = \dfrac{v}{f} = \dfrac{342 \text{ m/s}}{45 \times 10^3 \text{ Hz}} = 7.6 \times 10^{-3}$ m $= 7.6$ mm.

Example 9.2   Find the speed of sound in an aluminum rod.

Solution: Given: $Y_{Al} = 7.0 \times 10^{10}$ N/m² (Table 9.1), $\rho = 2.7 \times 10^3$ kg/m³ (Table 9.2)

   Find: v.

$$v = \sqrt{\frac{Y}{\rho}} = \sqrt{\frac{7.0 \times 10^{10} \text{ N/m}^2}{2.7 \times 10^3 \text{ kg/m}^3}} = 5.1 \times 10^3 \text{ m/s}.$$

---

3. Sound Intensity and Sound Intensity Level (Section 9.3)

Sound **intensity** is the rate of the sound energy transfer or the energy transported per unit time across a unit area: intensity $= \dfrac{\text{energy/time}}{\text{area}} = \dfrac{\text{power}}{\text{area}}$. The SI units of intensity are W/m^2.

The intensity of a point source of power P at a distance R from the source is given by $I = \dfrac{P}{A} = \dfrac{P}{4\pi R^2}$. Note that *the intensity is inversely proportional to the square of the distance from the point source.*

Sound intensity is perceived by the ear as **loudness**. On average, the human ear can detect sound waves (at 1 kHz) with an intensity as low as $I_o = 10^{-12}$ W/m^2 (I_o is called the **threshold of hearing**). At an intensity of $I_p = 1.0$ W/m^2 (I_p is called the **threshold of pain**) the sound is uncomfortably loud and may be painful to the ear. The ratio between the two intensities is $\dfrac{I_p}{I_o} = \dfrac{1.0 \ W/m^2}{10^{-12} \ W/m^2} = 10^{12}$, or 12 orders of magnitude. For a sound to be audible, it must have a frequency between 20 Hz and 20 kHz *and* have an intensity greater than I_o.

The **sound intensity level**, or **decibel level** (β) of a sound of intensity I is defined as $\beta = 10 \log \dfrac{I}{I_o}$, where $I_o = 10^{-12}$ W/m^2 is the threshold of hearing. At the threshold of hearing, $\beta = 10 \log \dfrac{I_o}{I_o} = 10 \log 1 = 0$ dB, and at the threshold of pain, $\beta = 10 \log \dfrac{1.0 \ W/m^2}{10^{-12} \ W/m^2} = 10 \log 10^{12} = 10(12) = 120$ dB. The 12 orders of magnitude of sound intensity is a difference of only 120 dB − 0 dB = 120 dB, on the decibel scale.

Note: Sound intensity and sound intensity level are two very different things. Intensity is a direct way measuring energy and is additive; that is, the sum of a 1.0 W/m^2 sound and a 2.0 W/m^2 sound will result in a sound of intensity 1.0 W/m^2 + 2.0 W/m^2 = 3.0 W/m^2. Intensity level is based on a logarithmic scale and therefore is not additive; that is, the sum of a 10 dB sound and a 20 dB sound will *not* make a sound of 10 dB + 20 dB ≠ 30 dB. Therefore, always use the definition of intensity level before answering any related questions.

Example 9.3 Your professor's lecturing voice has a power of about 0.50 mW. If this power is assumed to be uniformly distributed in all directions,

(a) what is the sound intensity at a distance of 5.00 m from the professor?

(b) what is the intensity level at a distance of 5.00 m from the professor?

(c) what will be the intensity level if the professor raises his voice so the intensity doubles to emphasize a concept?

Solution: Given: $R = 5.00$ m, $\quad P = 0.50$ mW $= 0.50 \times 0^{-3}$ W.

Find: (a) I (b) β (c) β for twice the intensity.

(a) $I = \dfrac{P}{4\pi R^2} = \dfrac{0.50 \times 10^{-3} \text{ W}}{4\pi(5.00 \text{ m})^2} = 1.6 \times 10^{-6}$ W/m^2.

(b) $\beta = 10 \log \dfrac{I}{I_0} = 10 \log \dfrac{1.6 \times 10^{-6} \text{ W/m}^2}{10^{-12} \text{ W/m}^2} = 10 \log 1.6 \times 10^{6} = 10(6.2) = 62$ dB.

(c) If the intensity doubles, the new intensity is $I = 2(1.6 \times 10^{-6} \text{ W/m}^2) = 3.2 \times 10^{-6}$ W/m^2.

Therefore, $\quad \beta = 10 \log \dfrac{3.2 \times 10^{-6} \text{ W/m}^2}{10^{-12} \text{ W/m}^2} = 10 \log 3.2 \times 10^{6} = 10(6.5) = 65$ dB.

Doubling the intensity increases the intensity level only by 65 dB $-$ 62 dB $= 3.0$ dB! This is always true because $10 \log 2I = 10 \,(\log I + \log 2) = 10 \,(\log I + 0.30) = 10 \log I + 3.0$.

Example 9.4 The intensity level generated by 25 computer keyboards at an on-line Internet company is 70 dB. What is the intensity level generated by one keyboard?

Solution: Given: $\beta\,(25) = 70$ dB, $\quad n = 25$.

Find: $\beta\,(1)$.

Intensity level is not additive (i.e., the intensity level of one keyboard is *not* $70/25 = 2.8$ dB). We first need to find the intensity generated by 25 keyboards, then the intensity of one keyboard, and finally the intensity level of one keyboard.

From $\beta = 10 \log \dfrac{I}{I_0}$, we have $\dfrac{\beta}{10} = \log \dfrac{I}{I_0}$, so $\dfrac{I}{I_0} = 10^{\beta/10}$ (because if $y = \log x$, then $x = 10^{y}$).

Therefore, $I(25) = I_0 10^{\beta/10} = (10^{-12} \text{ W/m}^2)10^{70/10} = (10^{-12} \text{ W/m}^2)10^{7} = 10^{-5}$ W/m^2, and the intensity generated by one keyboard is $I(1) = \dfrac{I(25)}{25} = \dfrac{10^{-5} \text{ W/m}^2}{25} = 4.0 \times 10^{-7}$ W/m^2 (intensity is additive).

Thus, $\beta\,(1) = 10 \log \dfrac{4.0 \times 10^{-7} \text{ W/m}^2}{10^{-12} \text{ W/m}^2} = 10 \log 4.0 \times 10^{5} = 56$ dB. (Are you surprised?)

---

4. Sound Phenomena (Section 9.4)

Because sound is a wave, it has all the wave characteristics. It can be *reflected, refracted,* and *diffracted,* that is, bounce off objects or surfaces, change in direction due to a medium or density change, and bend around corners or objects, respectively.

Sound waves *interfere* when they meet. There can be **constructive interference** or **destructive interference** depending on the **path-length difference** (ΔL) of the waves. If the path-length difference between two waves of the same frequency is zero or an integer (whole) number of wavelengths, $\Delta L = n\lambda$ with $n = 0, 1, 2, \ldots$, constructive interference (two crests or two troughs coincide) occurs. Conversely, if the path-length difference between two waves of the same frequency is an odd number of half-wavelengths, $\Delta L = m(\lambda/2)$ with $m = 1, 3, 5, \ldots$, destructive interference (crest and trough coincide) takes place. The **phase difference** $\Delta\theta$ is related to path-length difference by the simple relationship $\Delta\theta = \dfrac{2\pi}{\lambda}(\Delta L)$. In terms of the phase difference, the conditions for interference are

$\Delta\theta = n(2\pi)$, with $n = 0, 1, 2, \ldots$ for constructive interference;

$\Delta\theta = m(\pi)$, with $m = 1, 3, 5, \ldots$ for destructive interference.

Another interesting interference effect occurs when two tones of nearly the same frequency ($f_1 \approx f_2$) sound simultaneously. The ear senses pulsations in loudness known as **beats**. The **beat frequency** is equal to the difference between the two frequencies, or $f_b = |f_1 - f_2|$.

Example   9.5   A person stands between two loudspeakers driven by an identical source. Each speaker produces a tone with a frequency of 155 Hz on a day when the speed of sound is 341 m/s. The person is 1.65 m from one speaker and 4.95 m from the other speaker. What type of interference does the person sense?

Solution: Given: $f = 155$ Hz, $v = 341$ m/s, $L_1 = 1.65$ m, $L_2 = 4.96$ m.

Find: Interference type (constructive or destructive).

To determine what type interference the person senses, we need to find the path-length difference as a function of wavelength. From $v = \lambda f$, we have $\lambda = \dfrac{v}{f} = \dfrac{341 \text{ m/s}}{155 \text{ Hz}} = 220$ m.

The path-length difference is $\Delta L = L_2 - L_1 = 4.95$ m $- 1.65$ m $= 3.30$ m $= \frac{3}{2}(2.20$ m$) = \frac{3}{2}\lambda = 3(\lambda/2)$, so the path-length difference is an odd number of half-wavelengths. Therefore, the interference is destructive.

Example   9.6   A music tuner uses a 256-Hz tuning fork to tune the frequency of sound from a musical instrument. If the tuner hears a beat frequency of 2.0 Hz, what is the frequency of the sound produced by the instrument?

Solution: Given: $f_b = 2.0$ Hz, $f_1 = 256$ Hz.

               Find: f_2.

From $f_b = |f_1 - f_2|$, we have $f_2 = |f_1 \pm f_b|$ (Note the absolute value sign!).

Thus, $f_2 = |256$ Hz ± 2.0 Hz$| = 254$ Hz or 258 Hz.

There are two answers for f_2 because we do not know whetherthe tuning fork or the musical instrument has the higher frequency.

---

5.   The Doppler Effect (Section 9.5)

If there is relative motion between a sound source and an observer, the observer will detect a frequency that is different from the frequency of the source. This phenomenon is called the **Doppler effect**. Generally, if the source and the observer are moving toward each other, the observed frequency is higher than the source frequency; and if the source and the observer are moving away from each other, the observed frequency is lower than the source frequency.

For a stationary observer, the frequency observed f_o by the observer due to a moving source of frequency f_s is given by $f_o = \dfrac{v}{v \pm v_s} f_s = \dfrac{1}{1 \pm \dfrac{v_s}{v}} f_s$, where v_s is the speed of the source, v is the speed of sound, the minus sign

corresponds to the source moving toward a stationary observer, and the plus sign corresponds to the source moving away from a stationary observer.

For a stationary source of frequency f_s, the frequency observed f_o by an observer due to the moving observer is given by $f_o = \dfrac{v \pm v_o}{v} f_s = \left(1 \pm \dfrac{v_o}{v} \right) f_s$, where v_o is the speed of the observer, v is the speed of sound, the plus sign

corresponds to an observer moving toward the source, and the minus sign corresponds to an observer moving away from the source.

Note: For source moving, use $-$ for *toward*, and $+$ for *away from* observer.

            For observer moving, use $-$ for *away from*, and $+$ for *toward* the source. (Just opposite! Why?)

Objects (usually planes) traveling at supersonic (speed greater than the speed of sound) produce large pressure ridges or shock waves that give rise to the **sonic boom** heard when a supersonic aircraft passes. The ratio of the speed of the source v_s to the speed of sound v is called the **Mach number**: $M = \dfrac{v_s}{v}$, and $M > 1$ for supersonic speeds.

Example 9.7 The frequency of a train horn is 500 Hz. Assume the speed of sound in air is 340 m/s. What is the frequency heard by an observer if

(a) the observer is moving away from the stationary train with a speed of 30.0 m/s?

(b) the train is approaching the stationary observer with a speed of 30.0 m/s?

Solution: Given: $f_s = 500$ Hz, $v = 340$ m/s, (a) $v_o = 30.0$ m/s, (b) $v_s = 30.0$ m/s.

Find: (a) f_o (b) f_o.

(a) Because the observer is moving away from the source, we use the minus sign in $f_o = \dfrac{v \pm v_o}{v} f_s$:

$$f_o = \frac{v - v_o}{v} f_s = \frac{340 \text{ m/s} - 30.0 \text{ m/s}}{340 \text{ m/s}} (500 \text{ Hz}) = 456 \text{ Hz}.$$

(b) Because the train (the source) is approaching (toward), we use the minus sign in $f_o = \dfrac{v}{v \pm v_s} f_s$:

$$f_o = \frac{v}{v - v_s} f_s = \frac{340 \text{ m/s}}{340 \text{ m/s} - 30.0 \text{ m/s}} (500 \text{ Hz}) = 548 \text{ Hz}.$$

Example 9.8 The Concord supersonic airplane flies from the United States to Europe with a Mach number of 1.05 where the air temperature is 5.0°C. What is the speed of the plane?

Solution: Given: $M = 1.05$, $T_C = 5.0°C$.

Find: v_s.

The speed of sound in air is $v = (331 + 0.6T_C)$ m/s $= [331 + 0.6(5.0)]$ m/s $= 334$ m/s.

From $M = \dfrac{v_s}{v}$, we have $v_s = Mv = (1.05)(334 \text{ m/s}) = 351$ m/s.

6. Musical Instruments and Sound Characteristics (Section 9.6)

Stringed musical instruments produce notes by setting up transverse standing waves in strings with different fundamental frequencies. The harmonic series is given by $f_n = n\dfrac{v}{2L} = nf_1$ (for $n = 1, 2, 3, \ldots$),

where L is the length of the string.

Organ pipes and wind instruments produce notes by forming longitudinal standing waves in air columns. For an open organ pipe (open at both ends), the harmonic series is given by $f_n = n\dfrac{v}{2L} = nf_1$ (for $n = 1, 2, 3, \ldots$), where L is the length of the pipe. For a closed organ pipe (only one end closed and the other end open), the harmonic series is given by $f_m = m\dfrac{v}{4L} = mf_1$ (for $m = 1, 3, 5, \ldots$). Note the missing even harmonics in a closed pipe.

The secondary auditory effects of **loudness**, **pitch**, and **quality** are related to the physical wave properties of *intensity*, *frequency*, and *waveform* (harmonics), respectively.

Example 9.9   A 3.00-m-long pipe is in a room where the temperature is 20°C.

(a) What is the frequency of the fundamental if the pipe is open?

(b) What is the frequency of the second harmonic if the pipe is open?

(c) What is the frequency of the fundamental if the pipe is closed?

(d) What is the frequency of the second harmonic if the pipe is closed?

Solution: Given: $L = 3.00$ m, $T_C = 20°C$.

Find: (a) f_1 (open)   (b) f_2 (open)   (c) f_1 (closed)   (d) f_2 (closed).

The speed of sound in air is $v = (331 + 0.6T_C)$ m/s $= [331 + 0.6(20)]$ m/s $= 343$ m/s.

(a) For an open pipe, $f_n = n\dfrac{v}{2L} = nf_1$ (for $n = 1, 2, 3, \ldots$),

so $f_1 = 1\dfrac{v}{2L} = \dfrac{343 \text{ m/s}}{2(3.00 \text{ m})} = 57.2$ Hz.

(b) $f_2 = 2f_1 = 2(57.2 \text{ Hz}) = 114$ Hz.

(c) For a closed pipe, $f_m = m\dfrac{v}{4L} = mf_1$ (for $m = 1, 3, 5, \ldots$),

so $f_1 = 1\dfrac{v}{4L} = \dfrac{343 \text{ m/s}}{4(3.00 \text{ m})} = 28.6$ Hz.

(d) Even harmonics cannot exist in a closed pipe. There is no second harmonic.

III. Mathematical Summary

Speed of Sound	$v = (331 + 0.6T_C)$ m/s $\quad$ (9.1)	Calculates the speed of sound in air (in m/s).
Intensity of a Point Source	$I = \dfrac{P}{4\pi R^2}$ and $\dfrac{I_2}{I_1} = \left(\dfrac{R_1}{R_2}\right)^2 \quad$ (9.2)	Calculates the intensity of a point source as a function of distance from it.
Intensity Level (in decibels)	$\beta = 10 \log \dfrac{I}{I_0} \quad$ (9.4) where $I_0 = 10^{-12}$ W/m^2	Calculates the intensity level from intensity.
Phase Difference (ΔL is path-length difference)	$\Delta\theta = \dfrac{2\pi}{\lambda}(\Delta L) \quad$ (9.5)	Computes the phase difference from path-length difference ΔL.
Condition for Constructive Interference	$\Delta L = n\lambda \ (n = 0, 1, 2, 3, \ldots)$ $\quad$ (9.6)	Defines the condition for constructive interference.
Condition for Destructive Interference	$\Delta L = m\dfrac{\lambda}{2} \ (m = 1, 3, 5, \ldots)$ $\quad$ (9.7)	Defines the condition for destructive interference.
Beat Frequency	$F_b = |f_1 - f_2| \quad$ (9.8)	Calculates the beat frequency from two frequencies.
Doppler Effect: Source Moving	$f_o = \dfrac{v}{v \pm v_s} f_s = \dfrac{1}{1 \pm \dfrac{v_s}{v}} f_s$ v_s = speed of source v = speed of sound $\quad$ (9.11)	Relates observed frequency and source frequency. − for source moving toward stationary observer + for source moving away from stationary observer
Doppler Effect: Observer Moving	$f_o = \dfrac{v \pm v_o}{v} f_s = \left(1 \pm \dfrac{v_o}{v}\right) f_s$ v_o = speed of observer v = speed of sound $\quad$ (9.14)	Relates observed frequency and source frequency. + for observer moving toward stationary source − for observer moving away from stationary source
Angle for Conical Shock Wave	$\sin\theta = \dfrac{vt}{v_s t} = \dfrac{v}{v_s} = \dfrac{1}{M}$ $\quad$ (9.15)	Calculates the angle for conical shock wave of a plane moving with speed v_p, where M is the Mach number
Mach Number	$M = \dfrac{v_s}{v} \quad$ (9.16)	Defines the Mach number of a moving source.

Natural Frequencies of Organ Pipe Open at Both Ends	$f_n = n \dfrac{v}{2L} = nf_1$ $(n = 1, 2, 3, \ldots)$ (9.17)	Gives the natural frequencies of an open (both ends open) organ pipe.
Natural Frequencies of Organ Pipe Closed on One End	$f_n = m \dfrac{v}{4L} = mf_1$ $(n = 1, 3, 5, \ldots)$ (9.18)	Gives the natural frequencies of a closed (one end open) organ pipe.

IV.   Solutions of Selected Exercises and Paired Exercises

10.   (a) $v = (331 + 0.6T_C)$ m/s $= [331 + 0.6(10)]$ m/s $= \boxed{337 \text{ m/s}}$.

      (b) $v = [331 + 0.6(20)]$ m/s $= \boxed{343 \text{ m/s}}$.

16.   The speed of sound in water is $v = 1500$ m/s.

      From $v = \lambda f$, we have $f = \dfrac{v}{\lambda} = \dfrac{1500 \text{ m/s}}{3.0 \times 10^{-4} \text{ m}} = \boxed{5.0 \times 10^6 \text{ Hz}}$.

22. $T_C = \frac{5}{9}(T_F - 32) = \frac{5}{9}(72 - 32) = 22.22°C;$ $v_s = (331 + 0.6T_C)$ m/s $= [331 + 0.6(22.22)]$ m/s $= 344.3$ m/s.

      $\Delta t = \dfrac{d}{v_b} + \dfrac{d}{v_s} = d\left(\dfrac{1}{v_b} + \dfrac{1}{v_s}\right),$ so $d = \dfrac{\Delta t}{\dfrac{1}{v_b} + \dfrac{1}{v_s}} = \dfrac{1.00 \text{ s}}{\dfrac{1}{200 \text{ m/s}} + \dfrac{1}{344.3 \text{ m/s}}} = \boxed{127 \text{ m}}$.

25.   (a) The answer is $\boxed{\text{less than double}}$. This is because the total time is the sum of the time it takes for the stone to hit the ground (free-fall motion) and the time it takes sound to travel back that distance. Whereas the time for sound is directly proportional to the distance, the time for free fall is not. Because $d = \frac{1}{2}gt^2$, or

      $t = \sqrt{\dfrac{2d}{g}}$ (see Chapter 2), doubling the distance d will increase the time by a factor of only $\sqrt{2}$, i.e.; that is, it will increase but not double.

      (b) $v = (331 + 0.6T_C)$ m/s $= (331 + 0.6 \times 20)$ m/s $= 343$ m/s,

      so $4.80 \text{ s} = \dfrac{d}{343 \text{ m/s}} + \sqrt{\dfrac{2d}{g}} = \dfrac{d}{343 \text{ m/s}} + \sqrt{\dfrac{2d}{9.80 \text{ m/s}^2}}.$

      Or $(2.915 \times 10^{-3})(\sqrt{d})^2 + 0.4518(\sqrt{d}) - 4.8 = 0.$

      Solving, we get $\sqrt{d} = 9.98$, that is, $d = (\sqrt{d})^2 = (9.98)^2 = \boxed{1.0 \times 10^2 \text{ m}}$

      (c) $t = \dfrac{3(99.6 \text{ m})}{343 \text{ m/s}} + \sqrt{\dfrac{2(3 \times 99.6 \text{ m})}{9.80 \text{ m/s}^2}} = \boxed{8.7 \text{ s}}$.

32. (a) The sound intensity is $I = \dfrac{P}{4\pi R^2} = \dfrac{1.0 \text{ W}}{4\pi(3.0 \text{ m})^2} = \boxed{8.8 \times 10^{-3} \text{ W/m}^2}$.

(b) $I = \dfrac{1.0 \text{ W}}{4\pi(6.0 \text{ m})^2} = \boxed{2.2 \times 10^{-3} \text{ W/m}^2}$.

34. (a) The sound intensity level is $\beta = 10 \log \dfrac{I}{I_0} = 10 \log \dfrac{10^{-12} \text{ W/m}^2}{10^{-12} \text{ W/m}^2} = 10 \log 1 = \boxed{0}$.

(b) $\beta = 10 \log \dfrac{1 \text{ W/m}^2}{10^{-12} \text{ W/m}^2} = 10 \log 10^{12} = 10(12) = \boxed{120 \text{ dB}}$.

46. From $\beta = 10 \log \dfrac{I}{I_0}$, we have $\Delta\beta = \beta_2 - \beta_1 = 10 \log \dfrac{I_2}{I_0} - 10 \log \dfrac{I_1}{I_0} = 10 \log \dfrac{I_2}{I_1}$.

In the preceding calculation, we used $\log x - \log y = \log \dfrac{x}{y}$,

so $\dfrac{I_2}{I_1} = 10^{\Delta\beta/10} = 10^{-3}$. Also, $\dfrac{I_2}{I_1} = \dfrac{R_1^2}{R_2^2}$.

Therefore, $R_2 = \sqrt{\dfrac{I_1}{I_2}}\, R_1 = \sqrt{10^3}\,(10.0 \text{ m}) = \boxed{316 \text{ m}}$.

49. (a) From $\beta = 10 \log \dfrac{I}{I_0}$, we have

$I = 10^{\beta/10}\, I_0 = 10^{9.5}\,(10^{-12} \text{ W/m}^2) = \boxed{3.2 \times 10^{-3} \text{ W/m}^2}$.

(b) From Exercise 14.46, $\dfrac{I_2}{I_1} = 10^{\Delta\beta/10} = 10^{1.2} = \boxed{16}$.

64. The observer moves with a speed of 50 km/h = 13.9 m/s toward the source,

so $f_o = \dfrac{v + v_o}{v} f_s = \dfrac{331 \text{ m/s} + 13.9 \text{ m/s}}{331 \text{ m/s}}\,(800 \text{ Hz}) = \boxed{834 \text{ Hz}}$.

67. Because $f = \dfrac{v}{\lambda} = \dfrac{\sqrt{\dfrac{F}{\mu}}}{\lambda}$, f is proportional to $\sqrt{F}$,

so $\dfrac{f_2}{f_1} = \sqrt{\dfrac{F_2}{F_1}} = \sqrt{0.985} = 0.9925$. Therefore, $f_2 = 0.9925 f_1$,

or $f_b = |f_1 - f_2| = f_1 - f_2 = 0.0075 f_1 = (0.0075)(440 \text{ Hz}) = \boxed{3.3 \text{ Hz}}$.

71.   (a) The Mach number is $M = \dfrac{1}{\sin \theta} = \dfrac{1}{\sin 35°} = \boxed{1.74}$.

(b) Also, $M = \dfrac{v_s}{v}$, so $v_s = Mv = 1.74\{[331 + 0.6(-20)]\text{ m/s}\} = \boxed{555\text{ m/s}}$.

73.   When the source is approaching, $f_{oA} = \dfrac{v}{v - v_s} f_s$,   (1)

When the source is moving away, $f_{oM} = \dfrac{v}{v + v_s} f_s$ (2)

$\dfrac{\text{Eq. (2)}}{\text{Eq. (1)}}$ gives $\dfrac{f_{oM}}{f_{oA}} = \dfrac{v - v_s}{v + v_s}$,   so $f_{oM}(v + v_s) = f_{oA}(v - v_s)$.

Therefore, $v_s = \dfrac{(f_{oA} - f_{oM})v}{f_{oA} + f_{oM}} = \dfrac{(476\text{ Hz} - 404\text{ Hz})(343\text{ m/s})}{476\text{ Hz} + 404\text{ Hz}} = \boxed{28\text{ m/s}}$.

82.   (a) 378 Hz = 3(126 Hz), and 630 Hz = 5(126 Hz), so it is a $\boxed{\text{closed pipe}}$, because only odd harmonics can exist in a closed pipe. Had this been an open pipe, there would have been both odd and even harmonics.

(b) From $f_n = \dfrac{mv}{4L}$, we have $L = \dfrac{v}{4f_1} = \dfrac{340\text{ m/s}}{4(126\text{ Hz})} = \boxed{0.675\text{ m}}$; here we take $m = 1$.

85.   (a) For a closed pipe, $f_m = \dfrac{mv}{4L}$,   for $m = 1, 3, 5, \ldots$. Thus, f_2 $\boxed{\text{does not exist, only odd harmonics}}$.

(b) $f_3 = \dfrac{3v}{4L} = \dfrac{3(343\text{ m/s})}{4(0.900\text{ m})} = 285.8$ Hz. The distance between a node and an antinode is $\lambda/4$.

$\lambda = \dfrac{v}{f} = \dfrac{343\text{ m/s}}{285.8\text{ Hz}} = 1.20$ m, so the distance is (1.20 m)/4 = $\boxed{0.30\text{ m}}$

87.   (a) The position at the mouthpiece is an $\boxed{\text{antinode}}$ because it has the maximum vibration.

(b) For an open pipe, $f_n = \dfrac{mv}{2L}$,

so $L = \dfrac{mv}{2f_n} = \dfrac{(1)(343\text{ m/s})}{2(262\text{ Hz})} = \boxed{0.655\text{ m}}$.

(c) $L = \dfrac{(1)(343\text{ m/s})}{2(440\text{ Hz})} = \boxed{0.390\text{ m}}$.

93.   From $f_o = \dfrac{v + v_o}{v} f_s$, we have $v_o = \dfrac{f_o - f_s}{f_s} v = \dfrac{2f_s - f_s}{f_s} = v$, which is at the $\boxed{\text{speed of sound}}$.

V. Practice Quiz

1. An echo is heard 2.0 s from a cliff on a day the temperature is 15°C. Approximately how far is the cliff from the observer?

    (a) 85 m   (b) 170 m   (c) 340 m   (d) 680 m   (e) 1360 m

2. The third harmonic frequency in a pipe closed at one end is 330 Hz. What is the frequency of the fundamental?

    (a) 110 Hz   (b) 220 Hz   (c) 330 Hz   (d) 660 Hz   (e) 990 Hz

3. The intensity of a point source at a distance d from the source is I. What is the intensity at half the distance from the source?

    (a) $I/4$ (b) $I/2$ (c) I (d) $2I$ (e) $4I$

4. If the intensity level of a loudspeaker is 40 dB, what is the intensity level of two identical speakers?

    (a) 20 dB   (b) 37 dB   (c) 40 dB   (d) 43 dB   (e) 80 dB

5. Two tones have frequencies of 330 Hz and 332 Hz. What is the beat frequency?

    (a) 0 Hz   (b) 2 Hz   (c) 331 Hz   (d) 662 Hz   (e) none of the above

6. The third harmonic frequency of a pipe open at both ends is 300 Hz. What is the length of the pipe? (Assume the speed of sound is 340 m/s.)

    (a) 3.40 m   (b) 1.70 m   (c) 1.13 m   (d) 0.567 m   (e) 0.378 m

7. A sound source has a frequency of 500 Hz. If a listener moves at a speed of 30.0 m/s toward the source, what is the frequency heard by the listener? (The speed of sound is 340 m/s.)

    (a) 456 Hz   (b) 578 Hz   (c) 500 Hz   (d) 522 Hz   (e) 544 Hz

8. Two loudspeakers are placed side by side and driven by the same frequency of 500 Hz. If the distance from a person to one of the speakers is 5.00 m, and the person detects little or no sound, what is the distance from the person to the other speaker? (The speed of sound is 340 m/s.)

    (a) 7.72 m   (b) 8.06 m   (c) 8.40 m   (d) 9.08 m   (e) 5.00 m

9. The sound intensity level 5.0 m from a point source is 70 dB. What is the sound intensity level at a distance of 10.0 m from the source?

    (a) 17.5 dB   (b) 35 dB   (c) 64 dB   (d) 67 m   (e) 140 dB

10.   What is the frequency heard by a stationary observer when a train approaches with a speed of 30.0 m/s? The frequency of the train horn is 600 Hz. (The speed of sound is 340 m/s.)

   (a) 547 Hz   (b) 551 Hz   (c) 600 Hz   (d) 653 Hz   (e) 658 Hz

11.   If the Mach number of an airplane is 1.2, what is its speed expressed in terms of the speed of sound v?

   (a) 0.20v (b) 0.83v (c) v (d) 1.2v (e) 1.4v

12.   A closed pipe has a fundamental frequency of 517 Hz at 0°C. What is the fundamental frequency of the same pipe when the temperature is 20°C?

   (a) 345 Hz   (b) 498 Hz   (c) 517 Hz   (d) 536 Hz   (e) 862 Hz

Answers to Practice Quiz:

1. c 2. a 3. e 4. d 5. b 6. b 7. e 8. b 9. c 10. e 11. d 12. d

CHAPTER 10

Reflection and Refraction of Light

I. Chapter Objectives

Upon completion of this chapter, you should be able to:

1. define and explain the concept of wave fronts and rays.

2. explain the law of reflection and distinguish between regular (specular) and irregular (diffuse) reflections.

3. explain refraction in terms of Snell's law and the index of refraction, and give examples of refractive phenomena.

4. describe total internal reflection and understand fiber-optic applications.

5. explain dispersion and some of its effects.

II. Chapter Summary and Discussion

1. Wave Fronts and Rays (Section 10.1)

A **wave front** is the line (in two dimensions) or surface (in three dimensions) defined by adjacent portions of a wave that are in phase. For example, a point light source emits spherical wave fronts because the points having the same phase angle are on the surface of a sphere. For a parallel beam of light, the wave front is a **plane wave front**. The distance between adjacent wave fronts is the wavelength of the wave.

A **ray** is a line drawn perpendicular to a series of wave fronts and pointing in the direction of propagation of the wave. For a spherical wave, the rays are radially outward, and for a plane wave, they are parallel to one another. The use of wave fronts and rays in describing optical phenomena such as reflection and refraction is called **geometrical optics**.

2. Reflection (Section 10.2)

The **law of reflection** states that the **angle of incidence** (the angle between the incident ray and the normal) equals the **angle of reflection** (the angle between the reflected ray and the normal), $\theta_i = \theta_r$, where θ_i is the angle of incidence, and θ_r is the angle of reflection. The incident ray, the normal, and the reflected ray are always in the same plane.

Note: All angles are measured *from the normal* (*line perpendicular to the reflecting surface*).

Regular (specular) reflection occurs from smooth surfaces, with the reflected rays parallel to one another. **Irregular (diffuse) reflection** occurs from rough surfaces, with the reflected rays being at different angles.

Example 10.1   Two mirrors make an angle of 90° with each other. A ray is incident on mirror M_1 at an angle of 30° to the normal. Find the direction of the ray after it is reflected from mirrors M_1 and M_2.

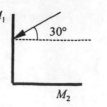

Solution:

All angles should be measured from the normal to the reflecting surface. The angle of incidence of the ray at M_1 is 30°. According to the law of reflection, the angle of reflection at M_1 is also 30°. From geometry, the angle of incidence at M_2 is 90° − 30° = 60°. Therefore, the angle of reflection at M_2 is also 60°, and the ray emerges parallel to the original incident ray.

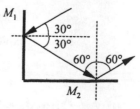

---

3.   Refraction (Section 10.3)

Refraction refers to the change in direction of a wave at a boundary where it passes from one medium into another as a result of different wave speeds in different media.

Snell's law relates the angle of incidence, θ_1, and angle of refraction θ_2, (the angle between the refracted ray and the normal) to the wave speeds in the respective media: $\dfrac{\sin \theta_1}{\sin \theta_2} = \dfrac{v_1}{v_2}$. The **index of refraction** of a medium is defined as the ratio of the speed of light in vacuum to its speed in that medium, $n = c/v$. Snell's law can be conveniently expressed in terms of the indices of refraction: $n_1 \sin \theta_1 = n_2 \sin \theta_2$. If the second medium is more optically dense ($n_2 > n_1$), then $\theta_1 > \theta_2$, or the refracted ray is bent toward the normal; if the second medium is less dense ($n_2 < n_1$), then $\theta_2 > \theta_1$, and the refracted ray is bent away from the normal.

When light travels from one medium to another the frequency remains constant, but the speed and wavelength change. In terms of wavelength, the index of refraction can be rewritten as $n = \lambda/\lambda_m$, where λ is the wavelength in vacuum, and λ_m is the wavelength in the medium.

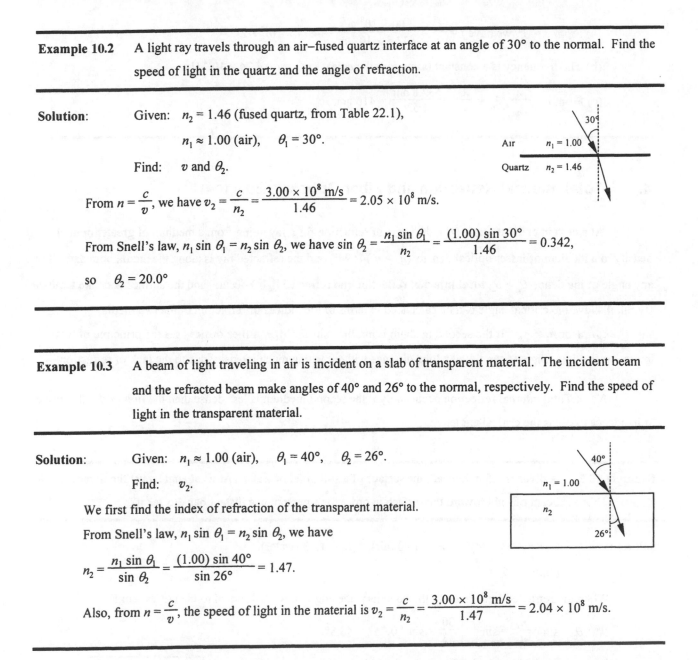

Note: Because the geometrical representation of light is used here, a diagram is very helpful (if not necessary) in solving problems. Again, all angles are measured from the normal to the interface boundary.

Example 10.2   A light ray travels through an air–fused quartz interface at an angle of 30° to the normal. Find the speed of light in the quartz and the angle of refraction.

Solution: Given: $n_2 = 1.46$ (fused quartz, from Table 22.1),

$n_1 \approx 1.00$ (air), $\theta_1 = 30°$.

Find: v and θ_2.

From $n = \dfrac{c}{v}$, we have $v_2 = \dfrac{c}{n_2} = \dfrac{3.00 \times 10^8 \text{ m/s}}{1.46} = 2.05 \times 10^8 \text{ m/s}.$

From Snell's law, $n_1 \sin \theta_1 = n_2 \sin \theta_2$, we have $\sin \theta_2 = \dfrac{n_1 \sin \theta_1}{n_2} = \dfrac{(1.00) \sin 30°}{1.46} = 0.342,$

so $\theta_2 = 20.0°$

Example 10.3   A beam of light traveling in air is incident on a slab of transparent material. The incident beam and the refracted beam make angles of 40° and 26° to the normal, respectively. Find the speed of light in the transparent material.

Solution: Given: $n_1 \approx 1.00$ (air), $\theta_1 = 40°$, $\theta_2 = 26°$.

Find: v_2.

We first find the index of refraction of the transparent material.

From Snell's law, $n_1 \sin \theta_1 = n_2 \sin \theta_2$, we have

$n_2 = \dfrac{n_1 \sin \theta_1}{\sin \theta_2} = \dfrac{(1.00) \sin 40°}{\sin 26°} = 1.47.$

Also, from $n = \dfrac{c}{v}$, the speed of light in the material is $v_2 = \dfrac{c}{n_2} = \dfrac{3.00 \times 10^8 \text{ m/s}}{1.47} = 2.04 \times 10^8 \text{ m/s}.$

Example 10.4   A light ray from a He-Ne laser has a wavelength of 632.8 nm and travels from air to crown glass.

(a) What is the frequency of the light in air?

(b) What is the frequency of the light in crown glass?

(c) What is the wavelength of light in crown glass?

Solution: Given: $n_2 = 1.52$ (crown glass from Table 22.1)

$$n_1 = 1.00 \text{ (air)}, \quad \lambda = 632.8 \text{ nm} = 632.8 \times 10^{-9} \text{ m}.$$

Find: (a) f (b) f_m (c) λ_m.

(a) From $c = \lambda f$, we have $f = \dfrac{c}{\lambda} = \dfrac{3.00 \times 10^8 \text{ m/s}}{632.8 \times 10^{-9} \text{ m}} = 4.74 \times 10^{14}$ Hz.

(b) The frequency is a constant (same for all media), so $f_m = f = 4.74 \times 10^{14}$ Hz.

(c) From $n = \dfrac{\lambda}{\lambda_m}$, $\lambda_m = \dfrac{\lambda}{n} = \dfrac{632.8 \text{ nm}}{1.52} = 416$ nm.

---

4.   Total Internal Reflection and Fiber Optics (Section 10.4)

At a certain **critical angle** (θ_c), the angle of refraction for a ray going from a medium of greater optical density to a medium of lesser optical density ($n_1 > n_2$) is 90°, and the refracted ray is along the media boundary. For any angle of incidence $\theta_1 > \theta_c$, **total internal reflection** (no refracted light) occurs, and the surface acts like a mirror. By Snell's law, the critical angle can be calculated in terms of the indices of refraction of the two media, $\sin \theta_c = n_2/n_1$ (for $n_1 > n_2$). If the second medium is air, then $\sin \theta_c = 1/n$. **Fiber optics** uses the principle of total internal reflection. Signals can travel a long distance without losing much intensity due to the lack of refraction.

Note: Total internal reflection occurs only if the second medium is less dense than the first *and* if the angle of incidence exceeds the critical angle.

Example 10.5   A diver is 1.5 m beneath the surface of a still pond of water. At what angle must the diver shine a beam of light toward the surface in order for a person on a distant bank to see it?

Solution: Given: $\theta_2 = 90°$, $n_2 = 1.00$ (air), $n_1 = 1.33$ (water).

Find: θ_1.

When the refracted light is along the boundary, the angle in water is equal to the critical angle.

$$\theta_1 = \theta_c = \sin^{-1} \frac{n_2}{n_1} = \sin^{-1} \frac{1.00}{1.33} = \sin^{-1} 0.752 = 48.8°.$$

Or from Snell's law, $n_1 \sin \theta_1 = n_2 \sin \theta_2$, we have

$$\sin \theta_1 = \frac{n_2 \sin \theta_2}{n_1} = \frac{(1.00) \sin 90°}{1.33} = 0.752. \text{ Thus, } \theta_1 = 48.8°.$$

For the light to reach the distant person, θ_1 has to be at or slightly below 48.8° so there is no total internal reflection. Can you explain why some fish-preying birds stay very low before they try to catch fish?

Example 10.6 A 45°–45° prism is a wedge-shaped object in which the two acute angles are 45° and very useful for changing the direction of light rays in optical devices. If a light ray is traveling through a glass prism according to the diagram shown, what is the minimum index of refraction of the glass?

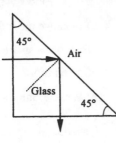

Solution: Given: $n_2 = 1.00$ (air), $\theta_c = 45°$. Find: n_1 (minimum).

There is no refracted ray beyond the glass–air boundary, so the light must be internally reflected. For total internal reflection to occur, the index of reflection n_1 must be greater than that of air. The minimum index of reflection corresponds to an angle of incidence of 45°, the critical angle.

$\sin \theta_c = \dfrac{n_2}{n_1}$, so the minimum index of refraction of the glass is

$$n_1 = \frac{n_2}{\sin \theta_c} = \frac{1.00}{\sin 45°} = 1.41.$$

5. Dispersion (Section 10.5)

Dispersion is the separation of multi-wavelength light into its component wavelengths when the light is refracted. This phenomenon is due to the fact that different wavelengths have slightly different speeds in a medium and therefore different indices of refraction. In most materials (so-called normal dispersion), longer wavelengths have smaller indices of refraction. According to Snell's law, different wavelengths will have different angles of refraction and are therefore separated. A rainbow is produced by refraction, dispersion, and total internal reflection within water droplets.

Example 10.7 A beam of white light strikes a piece of glass at a 70° angle (measured from the normal). A red light of wavelength 680 nm and a blue light of wavelength 430 nm emerge from the boundary after being dispersed. The index of refraction for the red light is 1.4505, and the index of refraction for the blue light is 1.4693.

(a) Which color of light is refracted more?

(b) What is the angle of refraction for each color?

(c) What is the angular separation between the two colors?

Solution: Given: $n_1 = 1.0000$ (air), $n_{2r} = 1.4505$, $n_{2b} = 1.4693$, $\theta_1 = 70°$.

Find: (b) θ_{2r} and θ_{2b} (c) $\Delta\theta$.

(a) Because the index of refraction of the blue light is greater, its angle of refraction is smaller (bent more toward the normal), and therefore it is refracted more.

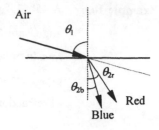

(b) We use Snell's law, $n_1 \sin \theta_1 = n_2 \sin \theta_2$.

For red: $\sin \theta_{2r} = \dfrac{n_1 \sin \theta_1}{n_{2r}} = \dfrac{(1.0000) \sin 70°}{1.4505} = 0.64784,$

so $\theta_{2r} = 40.379°$;

For blue: $\sin \theta_{2b} = \dfrac{(1.0000) \sin 70°}{1.4693} = 0.63955,$

so $\theta_{2b} = 39.758°$.

(c) The angular separation between the two colors is then

$\Delta\theta = \theta_{2r} - \theta_{2b} = 40.379° - 39.758° = 0.621°.$

III.   Mathematical Summary

Law of Reflection	$\theta_i = \theta_r$ (10.1)	Relates the angles of incidence and reflection.
Index of Refraction	$n = \dfrac{c}{v} = \dfrac{\lambda}{\lambda_m}$ (10.3, 10.4)	Defines the index of refraction of a material.
Snell's Law	$\dfrac{\sin \theta_1}{\sin \theta_2} = \dfrac{v_1}{v_2}$ (10.2) or $n_1 \sin \theta_1 = n_2 \sin \theta_2$ (10.5)	Relates the angles of incidence and refraction, and the speeds of light in the media (or indices of refraction).
Critical Angle at Boundary between Two Materials	$\sin \theta_c = \dfrac{n_2}{n_1}$, (10.6) where $n_1 > n_2$	Computes the critical angle between two materials for total internal reflection.

IV.   Solutions of Selected Exercises and Paired Exercises

11.   According to the law of reflection, $\theta_i = \theta_r = 32°$ from the normal,

.   so the angle between the surface and the beam is $90° - \theta_r = \boxed{58°}$.

14. (a) If the angle of incidence is β, the angle of reflection is also β, so the angle formed by the left mirror and the light reflecting off the left mirror is $90° - \beta$.

Then, the angle between the right mirror and the light incident on the right mirror is $180° - [(90° - \beta) + \alpha] = 90° + \beta - \alpha$.

Therefore the angle of incidence on the right mirror is

$90° - [90° + \beta - \alpha] = \alpha - \beta$.

Thus, the angle of reflection off the right mirror is also $\boxed{\alpha - \beta}$.

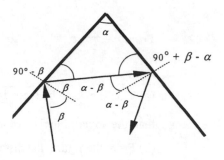

(b) For $\alpha = 60°$ and $\beta = 40°$, the angle of reflection off the right mirror is $\alpha - \beta = 60° - 40° = \boxed{20°}$.

17. We draw the ray diagram and assume the length and width of the square mirror to be a.

The area of a square is $A = a^2$, so $a = \sqrt{A} = \sqrt{900 \text{ cm}^2} = 30 \text{ cm} = 0.30 \text{ m}$.

We use similar triangles: $\dfrac{d + 0.45 \text{ m} + 0.45 \text{ m}}{8.50 \text{ m}} = \dfrac{0.45 \text{ m}}{0.30 \text{ m}}$.

Therefore, $d = \boxed{12 \text{ m}}$.

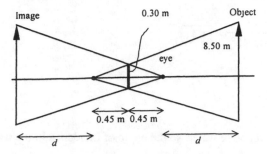

34. (a) According to Snell's law, the angle of refraction will be $\boxed{\text{less than}}$ the angle of incidence because water has a higher index of refraction.

(b) From $n_1 \sin \theta_1 = n_2 \sin \theta_2$, we have $\sin \theta_2 = \dfrac{n_1 \sin \theta_1}{n_2} = \dfrac{(1) \sin 60°}{1.33} = 0.651$,

so $\theta_2 = \boxed{41°}$.

39. From Snell's law, $n_1 \sin \theta_1 = n_2 \sin \theta_2$, we have $\sin \theta_1 = \dfrac{n_2 \sin \theta_2}{n_1} = \dfrac{(1.46) \sin 30°}{1} = 0.73$,

so $\theta_1 = 47°$.

Therefore, the angle of reflection is also $\boxed{47°}$ according to the law of reflection.

42.   From $n = \dfrac{c}{v}$, $v = \dfrac{c}{n}$, so $\dfrac{v_B}{v_A} = \dfrac{c/n_B}{c/n_A} = \dfrac{n_A}{n_B} = \dfrac{4/3}{5/4} = \boxed{\dfrac{16}{15}}$.

45.   (a) This is caused by $\boxed{\text{refraction}}$ of light in the water-air interface. The angle of refraction in air is greater

than the angle of incidence in water, so the object immersed in water appears closer to the surface.

(b) From the figure, the distance a is common to both d and d', and from trigonometry

$$\tan\theta_1 = \dfrac{a}{d'} \text{ and } \tan\theta_2 = \dfrac{a}{d}.$$

Combining these two equations to form a ratio, we obtain

$$\dfrac{d'}{d} = \dfrac{\tan\theta_2}{\tan\theta_1}, \text{ or } d' = \dfrac{\tan\theta_2}{\tan\theta_1}\,d.$$

If $\theta < 15°$, $\tan\theta \approx \sin\theta$, so $\dfrac{d'}{d} = \dfrac{\tan\theta_2}{\tan\theta_1} \approx \dfrac{\sin\theta_2}{\sin\theta_1} = \dfrac{1}{n}$ (Snell's law).

Therefore, $d' \approx \dfrac{d}{n}$.

47.   (a) This arrangement depends on $\boxed{\text{the indices of refraction of both}}$ media, because $\theta_c \geq \sin^{-1}\dfrac{n_2}{n_1}$.

(b) Air: $\theta_c \geq \sin^{-1}\dfrac{n_2}{n_1}$, so $n_1 \geq \dfrac{n_2}{\sin\theta_c} = \dfrac{1}{\sin 45°} = \boxed{1.41}$.

Water: $n_1 \geq \dfrac{n_2}{\sin\theta_c} = \dfrac{1.33}{\sin 45°} = \boxed{1.88}$.

52.   The setting is at zero altitude or 90° from the normal above water, so the angle of incidence in the water should be equal to the critical angle of

$$\theta_c = \sin^{-1}\dfrac{n_2}{n_1} = \sin^{-1}\dfrac{1}{1.33} = \sin^{-1} 0.752 = 48.8°.$$

Then, the angle to the surface is $90° - 48.8° = \boxed{41.2°}$.

57.   (a) $\theta_c = \sin^{-1}\dfrac{n_2}{n_1} = \sin^{-1}\dfrac{1}{1.60} = \boxed{38.7°} < 45°$,

so the answer is $\boxed{\text{no}}$, the beam is not transmitted but internally reflected.

(b) $\theta_c = \sin^{-1}\dfrac{n_2}{n_1} = \sin^{-1}\dfrac{1.20}{1.60} = 48.6° > 45°$,

so the beam is not internally reflected and is $\boxed{\text{transmitted}}$.

59. $\theta_2 = \tan^{-1} \dfrac{0.50\text{ m}}{0.75\text{ m}} = \tan^{-1} 0.667 = 33.7°; \quad n_1 \sin \theta_1 = n_2 \sin \theta_2,$

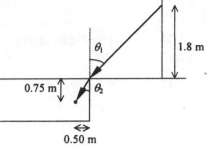

so $\sin \theta_1 = \dfrac{n_2 \sin \theta_2}{n_1} = \dfrac{(1.33) \sin 33.7°}{1} = 0.738.$

Therefore, $\theta_1 = 47.5°.$

Thus, $d = (1.8\text{ m}) \tan \theta_1 = (1.8\text{ m}) \tan 47.5° = \boxed{2.0\text{ m}}.$

69.   (a) $\boxed{\text{The angle of incidence is approximately zero}}$ and so there is no dispersion, because the angle of

refraction for all colors is also zero.

(b) $\boxed{\text{No}}$, as explained in (a). $\boxed{\text{No}}$, the speeds are different.

70.   (a) $\boxed{\text{Blue}}$ will experience more refraction, as its index of refraction is more different than that for red,

compared with the index of refraction of air. According to Snell's law, blue has a smaller angle of
refraction or deviates more from the angle of incidence.

(b) From Snell's law, $n_1 \sin \theta_1 = n_R \sin \theta_R = n_B \sin \theta_B$, we have

$\theta_R = \dfrac{n_1 \sin \theta_1}{n_R} = \dfrac{(1) \sin 37°}{1.515} = 0.3972,$ so $\theta_R = 23.406°.$

$\sin \theta_B = \dfrac{(1) \sin 37°}{1.523} = 0.3952.$ Therefore, $\theta_B = 23.275°.$

Thus, $\Delta \theta = \theta_R - \theta_B = 23.406° - 23.275° = \boxed{0.131°}.$

73.   (a) For the first air-prism interface,   (1) $\sin 80.0° = (1.400) \sin \theta_2,$

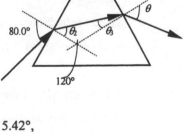

so $\theta_2 = \sin^{-1} 0.7034.$ Therefore, $\theta_2 = 44.70°.$

For the second prism-air interface,

$\theta_3 = 180° - (120° + \theta_2) = 60° - \theta_2 = 60° - 44.70° = 15.30°.$

$(1.400) \sin 15.30° = (1) \sin \theta,$ so $\theta = \sin^{-1} 0.3693 = 21.68° = \boxed{21.7°}.$

(b) For blue light, $\theta_2 = \sin^{-1} \dfrac{\sin 80.0°}{1.403} = 44.58°; \quad \theta_3 = 60° - 44.58° = 15.42°,$

so $\theta = \sin^{-1} [(1.403) \sin 15.42°] = 21.90°.$ Therefore $\Delta \theta = 21.90° - 21.68° = \boxed{0.22°}.$

(c) For blue light, $\theta_2 = \sin^{-1} \dfrac{\sin 80.0°}{1.405} = 44.50°.$ $\theta_3 = 60° - 44.50° = 15.50°,$

so $\theta = \sin^{-1} [(1.405) \sin 15.50°] = 22.05°.$ Therefore $\Delta \theta = 22.05° - 21.68° = \boxed{0.37°}.$

V. Practice Quiz

1. If the speed of light in a material is 2.13×10^8 m/s, what is its index of refraction?
   (a) 0.710   (b) 1.07   (c) 1.41   (d) 2.13   (e) 5.13

2. A light ray in air is incident on an air-glass interface at an angle of 45° and is refracted in the glass at an angle of 27° with the normal. What is the index of refraction of the glass?
   (a) 0.642   (b) 1.16   (c) 1.41   (d) 1.56   (e) 2.20

3. An optical fiber is made of clear plastic with index of refraction of $n = 1.50$. What is the minimum angle of incidence so total internal reflection can occur?
   (a) 23.4°   (b) 32.9°   (c) 38.3°   (d) 40.3°   (e) 41.8°

4. A certain kind of glass has an index of refraction of 1.65 for blue light and an index of refraction of 1.61 for red light. If a beam of white light (containing all colors) is incident at an angle of 30°, what is the angle between the refracted red and blue light?
   (a) 0.22°   (b) 0.35°   (c) 0.45°   (d) 1.90°   (e) 1.81°

5. A ray of white light, incident on a glass prism, is dispersed into its various color components. Which one of the following colors experiences the least refraction?
   (a) orange   (b) yellow   (c) red   (d) blue   (e) green

6. Which one of the following describes what will generally happen to a light ray incident on a glass-air boundary?
   (a) total reflection   (b) total refraction   (c) partial reflection, partial refraction
   (d) either (a) or (c)   (e) either (b) or (c)

7. Light enters water from air. The angle of refraction will be
   (a) greater than or equal to the angle of incidence.   (b) less than or equal to the angle of incidence.
   (c) equal to the angle of incidence.   (d) greater than the angle of incidence.
   (e) less than the angle of incidence.

8. Dispersion can be observed in
   (a) reflection   (b) refraction   (c) total internal reflection
   (d) all the preceding   (d) none of the preceding

9. A fiber-optic cable ($n = 1.50$) is submerged in water. What is the critical angle for light to stay inside the cable?

(a) 27.6°   (b) 41.8°   (c) 45.0°   (d) 62.5°   (e) 83.1°

10. An oil film ($n = 1.47$) floats on a water ($n = 1.33$) surface. If a ray of light is incident on the air-oil boundary at an angle of 37° to the normal, what is the angle of refraction at the oil-water boundary?

(a) 17.9°   (b) 24.2°   (c) 26.9°   (d) 33.0°   (e) 37.0°

11. The angle of incidence of a light ray entering water from air is 30°. What is the angle between the reflected ray and the refracted ray?

(a) 22°   (b) 52°   (c) 60°   (d) 68°   (e) 128°

8. A monochromatic light source emits a wavelength of 633 nm in air. When the light passes through a liquid, its wavelength decreases to 487 nm. What is the index of refraction of the liquid?

(a) 0.769   (b) 1.30   (c) 1.41   (d) 1.62   (e) 2.11

Answers to Practice Quiz:

1. c 2. d 3. e 4. c 5. c 6. d 7. e 8. b 9. b 10. d 11. c 12. b